Air Quality: EPA's 2013 Changes to the Particulate Matter (PM) Standard

Robert Esworthy
Specialist in Environmental Policy

January 23, 2013

Congressional Research Service

7-5700

www.crs.gov

R42934

CRS Report for Congress ———————————————————

Prepared for Members and Committees of Congress

Summary

On January 15, 2013, the Environmental Protection Agency (EPA) published a final rule revising the National Ambient Air Quality Standard (NAAQS) for particulate matter (PM). The revised air quality standards were completed pursuant to the Clean Air Act (CAA) and, in part, in response to a court order and consent agreement. Based on its review of scientific studies available since the agency's previous review in 2006, EPA determined that evidence continued to show associations between particulates in ambient air and numerous significant health problems, including aggravated asthma, chronic bronchitis, non-fatal heart attacks, and premature death. Populations shown to be most at risk include children, older adults, and those with heart and lung disease, and those of lower socioeconomic status. EPA's review of and revisions to the PM NAAQS has generated considerable debate and oversight in Congress.

The January 2013 revisions change the existing (2006) annual health-based ("primary") standard for "fine" particulate matter 2.5 micrometers or less in diameter (or $PM_{2.5}$), lowering the allowable average concentration of $PM_{2.5}$ in the air from the current level of 15 micrograms per cubic meter ($\mu g/m^3$) to a limit of 12 $\mu g/m^3$. The annual $PM_{2.5}$ NAAQS is set so as to address human health effects from chronic exposures to the pollutants. The existing "24-hour primary standard" for $PM_{2.5}$ that was reduced from 65 $\mu g/m^3$ to 35 $\mu g/m^3$ in 2006 was retained, as was the existing standard for larger, but still inhalable, "coarse" particles less than 10 micrometers in diameter, or PM_{10}. "Secondary" standards that provide protection against "welfare" (non-health) effects, such as ecological effects and material deterioration, are identical to the primary standards and the same as in 2006. The proposed rule published June 29, 2012, solicited comments on two options for a 24-hour $PM_{2.5}$ standard to improve visibility that were not adopted in the final rule.

EPA revised the Regulatory Impact Analysis (RIA) accompanying its June 2012 proposed rule in part in response to comments received regarding the agency's cost and benefit estimates. In its December 2012 RIA, EPA estimated that the potential "quantifiable" health benefits (2010 $) associated with attaining the PM standard would range from $4.0 billion to $9.1 billion, and costs (2010 $) would range from $53.0 million to $353.0 million. Some stakeholders and some Members continue to express concerns that cost impacts would be more significant than those estimated by EPA for those areas out of compliance with the new standards.

EPA's revisions to the PM NAAQS do not directly regulate emissions from specific sources, or compel installation of any pollution control equipment or measures, but indirectly could affect operations at industrial facilities and other sources throughout the United States. Revising PM NAAQS starts a process that includes a determination of areas in each state that exceed the standard and must, therefore, reduce pollutant concentrations to achieve it. Following determinations of these "nonattainment" areas based on multiple years of monitoring data and other factors, state and local governments must develop (or revise) State Implementation Plans (SIPs) outlining measures to attain the standard. These often involve promulgation of new regulations by states, and the issuance of revised air permits. The process typically takes several years. Based on statutory scheduling requirements, nonattainment designations for revised PM NAAQS would not be determined until the end of 2014, and states would have until at least 2020 to achieve compliance with the January 2013 revised $PM_{2.5}$ NAAQS.

Contents

Figures

Tables

Appendixes

Contacts

Introduction

On January 15, 2013, the Environmental Protection Agency (EPA) published a final rule in the *Federal Register* to strengthen the National Ambient Air Quality Standard (NAAQS) for particulate matter (PM),[1] intended to address potential health effects (including chronic respiratory disease and premature mortality) associated with short- and long-term exposure to particulate matter pursuant to the Clean Air Act (CAA).[2] The CAA, enacted in 1970 and amended in 1990, requires EPA to set minimum NAAQS for six "criteria air pollutants, including, ozone ("smog"), particulate material ("soot"), sulfur dioxides, nitrogen oxides, carbon monoxide, and lead. The law also requires EPA to evaluate each NAAQS every five years to determine whether it is adequately protective of human health and the environment, based on the most recent science.[3]

The EPA Administrator signed the final PM NAAQS rule on December 14, 2012, as per a June 6, 2012, order issued by the U.S. Court of Appeals for the District of Columbia Circuit in response to petitions filed by advocacy groups and 11 states,[4] and as agreed to in a September 4, 2012, consent decree.[5] EPA's most recent statutorily required review and proposal has generated controversy and national debate among a variety of stakeholders including industry groups, health and environmental advocacy groups, and states, as well as oversight in Congress. Similar controversy and debate transpired during the previous changes leading up to the existing PM NAAQS promulgated October 2006, and those established in 1997.

EPA published a proposed rule on June 29, 2012,[6] which started a nine-week public comment period that ran through August 31, 2012. EPA also held two public hearings for the proposal on July 17, 2012, in Philadelphia, PA, and July 19, 2012, in Sacramento, CA.[7] EPA reportedly received and considered more than 230,000 written comments in determining the final PM standard.

The June 2012 proposal and the January 2013 final PM NAAQS rule were the culmination of EPA's statutorily required review of the NAAQS under the CAA based on studies available through mid-2009 and recommendations of EPA staff and a scientific advisory panel (Clean Air Scientific Advisory Committee, or CASAC[8]) established by the CAA.[9] The agency initiated the

---

[1] The final rule and supporting documents are available on EPA's website *Particulate Matter (PM): Regulatory Actions*, http://www.epa.gov/pm/actions.html.

[2] Sections 108-109 of the Clean Air Act (CAA) govern the establishment, review, and revisions of the NAAQS (42 U.S.C. 7408 and 7409).

[3] Section 109(d)(1)) of the CAA.

[4] *American Lung Ass'n v. EPA*, D.D.C., No. 1:12-cv-243, order issued June 6, 2012.

[5] *American Lung Ass'n v. EPA*, D.D.C., No. 1:12-cv-243, order signed September 4, 2012. See also U.S. EPA, "Proposed Consent Decree," 77 *Federal Register* 38060, June 26, 2012, http://www.gpo.gov/fdsys/search/pagedetails.action?granuleId=2012-15603&packageId=FR-2012-06-26&acCode=FR, and *American Lung Ass'n v. EPA*, D.D.C., No. 1:12-cv-243, joint motion filed June 5, 2012.

[6] U.S. EPA, National Ambient Air Quality Standards for Particulate Matter, Proposed Rule, 77 *Federal Register* 38889-39055, June 29, 2012. The proposal as signed by EPA Administrator Lisa P. Jackson on June 14, 2012, and supporting documents are available on EPA's website *Particulate Matter (PM): Regulatory Actions*, http://www.epa.gov/pm/actions.html.

[7] U.S. EPA, Public Hearings for Proposed Rules—National Ambient Air Quality Standards for Particulate Matter, 77 *Federal Register* 39205, July 2, 2012.

[8] For information regarding the CASAC PM review panel and its activities and reports, see http://yosemite.epa.gov/sab/
(continued...)

---

review not long after the 2006 promulgation of the PM NAAQS.[10] EPA staff reassessed scientific studies considered in setting the 2006 PM NAAQS revisions, reviewed and analyzed extensive subsequent research, and considered public comments and recommendations of the CASAC.

Based on the scientific evidence and comments considered, EPA Administrator Lisa P. Jackson signed the final rule that would change the current standard primarily by lowering the annual health-based ("primary") standard for fine particles smaller than 2.5 microns ($PM_{2.5}$). In the final rule, the "secondary" standards that provide protection against "welfare" (non-health) effects, such as ecological effects and material deterioration, are identical to the primary standards, the same as in 2006. The final rule relies on the existing secondary 24-hour standard to protect against visibility impairment, and did not adopt a separate standard included among options in the June 2012 proposal. Also, as proposed,[11] the final rule did not modify the standards for inhalable "coarse" particles larger than 2.5 but smaller than 10 microns (PM_{10}). Some stakeholders in the agricultural community and some Members maintained a particular interest in EPA's consideration of the PM_{10} standards and potential impacts that revising the NAAQS may impose on the agricultural operations.[12]

As per statutory scheduling requirements under the CAA, the final designation of areas (primarily counties) as nonattainment for any revised PM standards would not be determined until the end of 2014, and states would have until at least 2020 to achieve compliance with the January 2013 PM NAAQS. In its revised Regulatory Impact Analysis (RIA) accompanying the final rule assessing the costs and benefits of proposed revisions to the PM NAAQS, EPA estimated that tightening the $PM_{2.5}$ annual standard would add further health benefits beyond those anticipated with the promulgation of the 2006 PM NAAQS.[13] Others have suggested that potential health benefits of tightening the PM NAAQS might be higher than EPA's estimates.[14] On the other hand, tighter standards could impose additional compliance requirements on communities, states, industry, and others, at what some stakeholders and Members contend will be a substantial economic cost. EPA expects that requirements and emission reductions associated with existing and recently promulgated federal regulations under the CAA will significantly allay impacts of complying

---

(...continued)

sabpeople.nsf/WebCommittees/CASAC.

[9] Section 109(d)(2) of the Clean Air Act.

[10] The current review was initiated with EPA's June 2007 general call for information, U.S. EPA, "Integrated Science Assessment for Particulate Matter: Call for Information," 72 *Federal Register* 35462, June 28, 2007. See also EPA's *Policy Assessment for the Review of the Particulate Matter National Ambient Air Quality Standards*, pp. 1-10 through 1-12, U.S. EPA Office of Air Quality Planning and Standards, Health and Environmental Impacts Division, EPA 452/R-11-003, April 2011, http://www.epa.gov/ttnnaaqs/standards/pm/data/20110419pmpafinal.pdf.

[11] See EPA's Fact Sheet, *Overview of EPA's Proposal to Revise the Air Quality Standards for Particle Pollution (Particulate Matter)*, http://www.epa.gov/pm/2012/fsoverview.pdf.

[12] See CRS Report R41622, *Environmental Regulation and Agriculture*, coordinated by Megan Stubbs.

[13] U.S. EPA, *Regulatory Impact Analysis for the Final Revisions to the National Ambient Air Quality Standards for Particulate Matter*, http://www.epa.gov/pm/2012/finalria.pdf. See also U.S. EPA, *Regulatory Impact Analysis for the Proposed Revisions to the National Ambient Air Quality Standards for Particulate Matter*, EPA 452/R-12-003, June 2012, http://www.epa.gov/ttn/ecas/regdata/RIAs/PMRIACombinedFile_Bookmarked.pdf. The RIA and supporting documents are available in the public docket, Docket No. EPA-HQ-OAR-2010-0955, http://www.regulations.gov/#!searchResults;rpp=25;po=0;s=EPA-HQ-OAR-2010-0955.

[14] For an example, see *Health Benefits of Alternative $PM_{2.5}$ Standards*, Donald McCubbin, Ph.D., prepared for the American Lung Association, Clean Air Task Force and Earthjustice, July 2011, http://earthjustice.org/sites/default/files/Health-Benefits-Alternative-PM2.5-Standards.pdf.

---

with the revised PM standards, and anticipates that virtually all counties will meet the standards as promulgated in 2020.

Several recent and pending EPA regulations implementing the various pollution control statutes enacted by Congress garnered vigorous oversight during the 112th Congress.[15] Members expressed concerns in hearings, through bipartisan letters commenting on proposed regulations, and through introduced legislation that would delay, limit, or prevent certain EPA actions. Particular attention was focused on EPA's implementation of the CAA. Because of health and cost implications, NAAQS decisions historically have been the source of significant concern to some in Congress. The evolution and development of the PM NAAQS, in particular, have been the subject of extensive oversight. During the 112th Congress, some Members expressed concerns in hearings, letters to the Administrator, and proposed legislation in anticipation of potential changes to the PM NAAQS, and the January 2013 final rule is expected to generate further oversight. Some Members[16] and industry stakeholders had urged EPA to delay the final rule, while conversely, others, including some states[17] and various environmental and public health advocacy groups, urged timely completion of a tighter standard. Changes to the NAAQS historically have triggered litigation alleging the standards are too stringent or not stringent enough, and often resulted in delays in implementation.

This CRS report summarizes EPA's January 15, 2013, final and June 2012 proposed changes to the PM NAAQS and includes comparisons with previous (1997 and 2006) promulgated and proposed standards. Key actions leading up to the agency's determination, and potential issues and concerns associated with changing the $PM_{2.5}$ annual standard, are also highlighted. For more information regarding issues and implementation of the $PM_{2.5}$ NAAQS promulgated in 2006, see CRS Report RL34762, *The National Ambient Air Quality Standards (NAAQS) for Particulate Matter (PM): EPA's 2006 Revisions and Associated Issues*, by Robert Esworthy, and CRS Report R40096, *2006 National Ambient Air Quality Standards (NAAQS) for Fine Particulate Matter (PM2.5): Designating Nonattainment Areas*, by Robert Esworthy.

Background

Particulate matter is one of six "criteria pollutants" for which EPA has promulgated NAAQS under the CAA.[18] The others are ozone ("smog"), nitrogen oxides (NO_x),[19] sulfur oxides (SO_x, or, specifically, SO_2), carbon monoxide (CO), and lead (Pb).

$PM_{2.5}$ can be emitted directly from vehicles, smokestacks, and fires but can also form in reactions in the atmosphere from gaseous precursors, including sulfur oxides, nitrogen oxides, and volatile

---

[15] See CRS Report R41561, *EPA Regulations: Too Much, Too Little, or On Track?*, by James E. McCarthy and Claudia Copeland.

[16] See November 21, 2012, letter from 47 Members of the House of Representatives to the U.S. EPA Administrator, http://latta.house.gov/uploadedfiles/2012_11_29_final_pm2_5_letter_signed_w_attchmt.pdf. Also see press release available on Representative Bob Latta's website at http://latta.house.gov/news/documentsingle.aspx?DocumentID= 314585.

[17] See December 6, 2012, letter from nine State Attorneys General to the Acting Administrator of the Office of Information and Regulatory Affairs, the White House Office of Management and Budget, http://www.eenews.net/ assets/2012/12/10/document_gw_02.pdf.

[18] 42 U.S.C. 7408(a)(1).

[19] The NAAQS is for NO_2; nitrogen gases that are ozone precursors are referred to as NOx.

organics occurring naturally or as emissions typically associated with gasoline and diesel engine exhaust, and from utility and other industrial processes. PM_{10} (or coarse PM) is an indicator used in the NAAQS to provide protection from slightly larger (in the range of 2.5 to 10 microns or thoracic "coarse" particles), but still inhalable particles that penetrate into the trachea, bronchi, and deep lungs. These particles are often associated with dust from paved and unpaved roads, construction and demolition operations (including mining), and sometimes with certain industrial processes and agriculture operations, as well as biomass burning.

Establishing NAAQS does not directly limit emissions; rather, it represents the EPA Administrator's formal judgment regarding the concentration of a pollutant in ambient air that will protect public health with an "*adequate margin of safety*." Under Sections 108-109 of the CAA,[20] Congress mandated that EPA set national ambient (outdoor) air quality standards for pollutants whose emissions "may reasonably be anticipated to endanger public health (primary standards) or welfare[21] (secondary standards)" and "the presence of which in the ambient air results from numerous or diverse mobile or stationary sources." The process for setting and revising NAAQS consists of the statutory steps incorporated in the CAA over a series of amendments. Several other steps have also been added by EPA, by executive orders, and by subsequent regulatory reform enactments by the Congress.

Section 109(d)(1)) of the CAA requires EPA to review the criteria that serve as the basis for the NAAQS for each covered pollutant every five years, to either reaffirm or modify previously established NAAQS. Prior to the January 2013 revisions, EPA has revised the PM NAAQS three times, in 1987, 1997, and October 2006, to ensure that the standards continue to provide adequate protection for public health and welfare.[22]

A February 24, 2009, decision by the U.S. Court of Appeals for the District of Columbia Circuit had remanded elements of EPA's decisions as promulgated in October 2006, in particular the decision not to tighten the primary annual NAAQS for $PM_{2.5}$, to the agency for further consideration but did not vacate the revised standard nor set a specific timeline. The decision was in response to petitions filed in the D.C. Circuit by 13 states, industry, agriculture, business, and environmental and public health advocacy groups, challenging certain aspects of EPA's revisions for both $PM_{2.5}$ and PM_{10}. The D.C. Circuit granted the petitions in part with regard to the $PM_{2.5}$ annual standard and the secondary standards for $PM_{2.5}$ and PM_{10} (including visibility impairment), denying other challenges.[23]

---

[20] 42 U.S.C. 7408(a)(1).

[21] The use of public welfare in the CAA "includes, but is not limited to, effects on soils, water, crops, vegetation, manmade materials, animals, wildlife, weather, visibility, and climate, damage to and deterioration of property, and hazards to transportation, as well as effects on economic values and on personal comfort and well-being, whether caused by transformation, conversion, or combination with other air pollutants" (42 U.S.C. 7602(h)).

[22] Beginning in 1971, regulation and monitoring of particulate matter under the CAA focused primarily on total suspended particles (TSP) and, eventually in 1987, on coarse particles equal to or less than 10 micrometers in diameter (PM_{10}). EPA revised the particulates standards in 1997 to provide separate requirements for fine particulate matter ($PM_{2.5}$). See EPA's "Particulate Matter (PM) Standards—Table of Historical PM NAAQS" at http://www.epa.gov/ttn/naaqs/standards/pm/s_pm_history.html.

[23] For a more detailed discussion regarding the petitions see section entitled "Petitions Challenging the 2006 PM NAAQS and the D.C. Circuit's February 29, 2009, Decision" in CRS Report RL34762, *The National Ambient Air Quality Standards (NAAQS) for Particulate Matter (PM): EPA's 2006 Revisions and Associated Issues*, by Robert Esworthy.

Concerned with delays in EPA's schedule for proposing revisions to the 2006 PM NAAQS, the American Lung Association and the National Parks Conservation Association, and nine states separately filed petitions with the D.C. Circuit in November 2011 urging the court to order EPA's immediate compliance with the February 2009 remand. Subsequently, in February 2012 the two organizations sued EPA in the D.C. Circuit for failing to fulfill their statutory duty to review the October 2006 PM NAAQS within five years,[24] and a coalition of 11 states filed a similar suit with the U.S. District Court Southern District of New York.[25] In response, the D.C. Circuit initially directed EPA to sign a proposed rule concerning its decision regarding revisions to the PM NAAQS by June 7, 2012, and following a motion filed by the agency, amended the deadline to June 14, 2012.[26] As part of a September 4, 2012, consent decree, EPA agreed to finalize revisions to the PM NAAQS by December 14, 2012.[27]

Promulgation of a revised NAAQS, such as the PM NAAQS, initiates a series of statutorily required actions, ultimately culminating in issuance of permits pursuant to state regulations in a State Implementation Plan (SIP). The first step is designation of attainment and nonattainment areas, based on the accumulated results of ambient air monitoring and modeling data. States first propose to designate certain geographic areas (e.g., counties) as either "attainment" or "nonattainment," depending on whether the data indicate the concentrations of pollutants will be below or above the NAAQS. After extensive dialogue with state officials, EPA either approves the proposed attainment and nonattainment areas, or sends back to states proposed revisions. EPA and states generally come to an agreement about the area designations. Following this designation, approved by EPA, states then develop a SIP, which consists essentially of state regulations to be implemented by states that would affect the state emissions inventory, and therefore the expected or modeled concentrations of air pollutants. After approval of the SIP as being adequate to control air pollution and reduce the ambient air pollutant concentrations in designated nonattainment areas, the states then issue permits (new or modified) for facilities whose emissions affect the air in designated nonattainment areas.

EPA's January 2013 Final Changes to the PM NAAQS

EPA's 1997 revisions to the PM NAAQS[28] revised the standards focused on particles smaller than 10 microns (PM_{10} or coarse particles) established in 1987,[29] and introduced standards for "fine" particles smaller than 2.5 microns ($PM_{2.5}$) for the first time. The primary (health protection) PM NAAQS as revised in 2006 include an *annual* and a *daily* (24-hour) limit for $PM_{2.5}$, but only a daily limit for PM_{10}. To attain the $PM_{2.5}$ annual standard, the three-year average of the weighted annual arithmetic mean $PM_{2.5}$ concentration at each monitor within an area must not exceed the maximum limit set by the agency. The 24-hour standards are a concentration-based percentile

---

[24] *American Lung Ass'n v. EPA*, D.D.C., No. 1:12-cv-243, filed February 14, 2012.

[25] *States of New York, California, Connecticut, Delaware, Maryland, New Mexico, Oregon, Rhode Island, Vermont, and Washington, and Commonwealth of Massachusetts v. EPA*, D.S. N.Y., 12 CIV 1064, filed February 10, 2012, http://www.atg.state.vt.us/assets/files/NY%20v%20EPA%20Complaint%20(2-10-12).pdf.

[26] See footnote 4.

[27] See footnote 5.

[28] 62 *Federal Register* 38652-38896, July 18, 1997.

[29] PM_{10} NAAQS were promulgated in 1987, 52 *Federal Register* 24640, July 1, 1987.

form,[30] indicating the percent of the time that a monitoring station can exceed the standard. For instance, a 98th percentile 24-hour standard indicates that a monitoring station can exceed the standard 2% of the time during the year. For $PM_{2.5}$ and PM_{10}, the secondary NAAQS, which are set at a level "requisite to protect the public welfare," are the same as the primary standards.

In the final rule published by EPA on January 15, 2013, the $PM_{2.5}$ and PM_{10} standards and other implementation changes are as follows:[31]

Primary (Public Health) PM Standards

- **$PM_{2.5}$:** EPA revised the *annual* standard, which currently is 15 micrograms per cubic meter ($\mu g/m^3$), by setting a new limit of 12 $\mu g/m^3$ (the proposal included an optional limit of 13 $\mu g/m^3$ and solicited comment for 11 $\mu g/m^3$); compliance with the "annual" standard is determined by whether the three-year average of its annual average $PM_{2.5}$ concentration (at each monitoring site in the area) is less than or equal to 12 $\mu g/m^3$; as proposed, EPA retained the *daily* (24-hour) standard at 35 $\mu g/m^3$ based on the current three-year average of the 98th percentile of 24-hour $PM_{2.5}$ concentrations as established in 2006.

- **PM_{10}:** As proposed, EPA retained the current *daily* standard of no more than one exceedance of concentrations of 150 $\mu g/m^3$ per year on average over three years; there is no current *annual* standard for PM_{10} (the previous annual maximum concentration standard of 50 $\mu g/m^3$ was eliminated by EPA in 2006).[32]

Secondary (Welfare) PM Standards

- **$PM_{2.5}$ and PM_{10}:** As proposed, secondary (welfare) NAAQS are the same as the primary standards, the same correlations as the 2006 PM NAAQS, with the exception of visibility impairment associated with $PM_{2.5}$.

- **$PM_{2.5}$ Visibility Impairment:** The final rule did not add a distinct secondary standard as proposed, defined in terms of a $PM_{2.5}$ visibility index based on speciated[33] $PM_{2.5}$ mass concentrations and relative humidity data to calculate light extinction on a deciview (dv) scale[34] similar to the current Regional Haze Program.[35] Specifically, the proposal would have set a 24-hour averaging time of

---

[30] "The "form" of a standard defines the air quality statistic that is to be compared to the level of the standard in determining whether an area attains that standard." 77 *Federal Register* 38954, June 29, 2012.

[31] See footnote 1.

[32] Based on the findings in the EPA PM criteria document and staff paper, and the CASAC's concurrence, that the studies reviewed do not provide sufficient evidence regarding *long-term* exposure to warrant continuation of an annual standard. See 71 *Federal Register* 2653, *Section III. Rationale for Proposed Decision on Primary PM_{10} Standards,* January 17, 2006.

[33] Includes a measure of $PM_{2.5}$ mass, elements, ions, and carbon species. See EPA's laboratory standard operating procedures (SOPs) for $PM_{2.5}$ chemical speciation at http://www.epa.gov/ttnamti1/specsop.html.

[34] "The deciview scale is frequently used in the scientific and regulatory literature on visibility. This metric describes changes in uniform light extinction that can be perceived by a human observer. One deciview represents the minimal perceptible change in visibility to the human eye," 77 *Federal Register* 39043, June 29, 2012. A "deciview is a yardstick for measuring visibility: the higher the deciview level, the hazier the air appears," U.S. EPA, Fact Sheet: *Revised Air Quality Standards for Particle Pollution and Updates to the Air Quality Index (AQI)*, http://www.epa.gov/pm/2012/decfsstandards.pdf.

[35] See U.S. EPA, "EPA's Regional Haze Program," http://www.epa.gov/visibility/program.html.

---

30 or 28 deciviews (dv) based on a 90th percentile form over three years. EPA also sought comment on alternative levels (down to 25 dv) and averaging times (e.g., 4 hours). Based on public comment and further analysis of air quality monitoring data, EPA concluded that the current secondary standard would provide visibility protection greater than or equal to 30 dv.[36]

Implementation Changes

- **Monitoring:**[37] As proposed, updates several aspects of monitoring regulations including requiring relocating a small number of $PM_{2.5}$ monitors[38] to be collocated with measurements of other criteria pollutants (e.g., nitrogen dioxide (NO_2) and carbon monoxide (CO)) near-roadway monitoring so as to ensure these monitors are at one location in each urban area with a population of 1 million or more, and to be phased in starting with the largest areas (2.5 million or more populations) by January 1, 2015, and extended to the remainder of areas by January 1, 2017. Includes the use data from existing Chemical Speciation Network or the EPA/National Park Service IMPROVE monitoring network to determine whether an area meets the proposed secondary visibility index standard for $PM_{2.5}$. No changes to PM_{10} monitoring.

- **Air Quality Index (AQI):** As proposed, updates the AQI (EPA's color-coded tool for informing the public about air quality and associated measures for reducing risks of exposure) for $PM_{2.5}$ by changing the upper end range for "Good" category (an index value of 50) on the overall scale (0 to 500 based on conversion of $PM_{2.5}$ concentrations) to the level of the revised annual $PM_{2.5}$ standard (12 $\mu g/m^3$). Also as proposed, EPA is setting the 100 value of the index scale ("Moderate") at the level of the current 24-hour $PM_{2.5}$ standard, which is 35 $\mu g/m,^3$ and the AQI of 150 ("Unhealthy Sensitive Groups") at 55 $\mu g/m^3$. The current upper end for the "Hazardous" (500), "Unhealthy" (200) and "Very Unhealthy" (300) AQIs are retained.[39]

- **Prevention of Significant Deterioration (PSD):**[40] EPA revised the PSD permitting program (rules) with respect to the revised PM NAAQS so as not to "unreasonably delay" pending permits and establish a "grandfather" provision for permit applications if: the permitting agency deems an application complete by December 14, 2012; or public notice for a draft permit or preliminary determination has been published (for public comment) no later than the effective

---

[36] See footnote 34.

[37] See EPA Fact Sheet: *EPA's Revised Air Quality Standards for Particle Pollution: Monitoring, Designations and Permitting Requirements*, http://www.epa.gov/pm/2012/decfsimp.pdf. See also EPA Fact Sheet: *EPA's Proposal to Update the Air Quality Standards for Particle Pollution: Monitoring, Designations and Permitting Requirements*, http://www.epa.gov/airquality/particlepollution/2012/fsimp.pdf.

[38] EPA indicated that it is not increasing the size of the current $PM_{2.5}$ monitoring network of about 900 monitors, but anticipates that states will be able to relocate roughly 52 existing monitors to meet the near-roadway requirement; see previous footnote.

[39] U.S. EPA, Fact Sheet: *See EPA Fact Sheet: Revised Air Quality Standards for Particle Pollution and Updates to the Air Quality Index (AQI)*, http://www.epa.gov/pm/2012/decfsstandards.pdf. See also EPA Fact Sheet: *Summary of Proposed Improvements to the Air Quality Standards for Particle Pollution and Updates to the Air Quality Index (AQI)*, http://www.epa.gov/pm/pdfs/PMNAAQSProposalSTANDARDSAQI61412FINALUPDATED.pdf.

[40] See footnote 37.

date of revised PM NAAQS (60 days after January 15, 2013, publication in the *Federal Register*). This provision would not apply to NAAQS for other criteria pollutants and permits not meeting these criteria would have to demonstrate compliance with the revised standards once they are finalized.

Comparison of the January 2013 Revised PM2.5 Standards with Previous Promulgated and Proposed Alternative PM Standards

The final PM$_{2.5}$ daily standard established in 2006 was among the less stringent within the range of alternative levels recommended by EPA staff, and the annual standard is not as stringent as the standard recommended by the CASAC. The decision to retain the annual PM$_{2.5}$ standard was also less than recommended. **Table 1** below shows the January 2013 revised PM$_{2.5}$ annual standard in comparison to the June 2012 proposed options and to the annual and daily standards for 1997 and 2006 promulgated standards, and alternative levels recommended prior to the 2006 final revisions.

Table 1. Promulgated, Proposed, and Alternative PM2.5 Primary (Health) National Ambient Air Quality Standards (NAAQS)

PM2.5 NAAQS Options	24-hour Primary	Annual Primary
	micrograms per cubic meter = µg/m³	
1997 Promulgated PM NAAQS	65 µg/m³	15 µg/m³
CASAC Recommendation (June 2005)	35-30 µg/m³	14-13 µg/m³
EPA Final "Staff Paper" (Dec. 2005)	35-25 µg/m³	15 µg/m³
	or	
	40-30 µg/m³	14-12 µg/m³
Dec. 2005 Proposed PM NAAQS Rule	35 µg/m³	15 µg/m³
2006 Promulgated PM NAAQS	35 µg/m³	15 µg/m³
CASAC Recommendation (August 2010)	35-30 µg/m³	13-11 µg/m³
EPA Final "Staff Paper" (April 2011)	35-30 µg/m³	13-11 µg/m³
2012 Proposed Rule (June 2012)	35 µg/m³	13-12 µg/m³ (EPA also solicited comments for a limit of 11 µg/m³)
January 15, 2013, Final Rule	35 µg/m³	12 µg/m³

Source: Prepared by the Congressional Research Service (CRS) with information from EPA's January 15, 2013, final rule and June 2012 proposal and related technical documents, and the December 2006 promulgated PM NAAQS and supporting technical and policy documents (http://www.epa.gov/air/particles/actions.html).

Note: PM2.5 = "fine" particulate matter 2.5 micrometers or less in diameter.

Review Process Leading Up to the January 2013 Revised PM NAAQS

The CAA as enacted includes specific requirements for a multistage process to ensure the scientific integrity under which NAAQS are set, laying the groundwork for the Administrator's determination of the standard, and the procedural process for promulgating the standard.[41] Primary NAAQS, as described in Section 109(b)(1), were to be "ambient air quality standards the attainment and maintenance of which in the judgment of the Administrator, based on such criteria and allowing an adequate margin of safety, are requisite to protect the public health."

Based on this premise, the CAA specifies the criterion to be used by the Administrator in deciding on the final standard, including preparation of a "criteria document" that summarizes scientific information assessed. The act also requires the establishment and role of an independent advisory committee (CASAC[42]) to review EPA's supporting scientific documents, and the timeline for completing specific actions. EPA administratively added the preparation of a "staff paper" that summarizes the criteria document and lays out policy options. This EPA document typically serves as the basis for CASAC review and comment. EPA revised certain aspects (not including reinstating the closure letter) of the CASAC review process most recently in May 2009.[43] In addition, Executive Order 12866 requires a Regulatory Impact Analysis (RIA), although the economic impact analysis is essentially only for informational purposes and cannot be directly considered as part of the decision in determining the NAAQS.[44]

Beginning June 2007 with its general call for information,[45] EPA initiated the current PM NAAQS review, which culminated in assessments of the scientific research and risk analyses, and ultimately the April 2011 publication of the staff's final *Policy Assessment for the Review of the Particulate Matter National Ambient Air Quality Standards (or PM Policy Assessment).*[46] The staff paper presented the staff conclusions and recommendations on the elements of the PM standard based on evaluation of the policy implications of the scientific evidence contained in the criteria document and the results of quantitative analyses (e.g., air quality analyses, human health

---

[41] For a detailed overview of the NAAQS process see CRS Report 97-722, *Air Quality Standards: The Decisionmaking Process.*

[42] For general information regarding the CASAC as well as the CASAC panel for the PM NAAQS review, see *EPA Clean Air Advisory Committee (CASAC)* website http://yosemite.epa.gov/sab/sabpeople.nsf/WebCommittees/CASAC.

[43] For EPA's most recent revisions to the CASAC review process, see the May 21, 2009, memorandum from Administrator Lisa P. Jackson to Dr. Jonathan Samet, CASAC Chair, and to Elizabeth Craig, Acting EPA Administrator for Air and Radon, and Lek Kadeli, Acting Administrator for Research and Development, http://yosemite.epa.gov/sab/sabproduct.nsf/WebCASAC/NewNAAQSProcess?OpenDocument.

[44] The CAA directs the EPA Administrator to protect public health *with an adequate margin of safety.* This language has been interpreted, both by the agency and by the courts, as requiring standards based on a review of the health impacts, without consideration of the costs, technological feasibility, or other non-health criteria. Costs and feasibility are generally taken into account in NAAQS implementation (a process that is primarily a state responsibility). With regard to the non-relevance of cost considerations, see generally Whitman v. American Trucking Associations, 531 U.S. 457, 465-472, 475-76 (2001).

[45] U.S. EPA, "Integrated Science Assessment for Particulate Matter: Call for Information," 72 *Federal Register* 35462, June 28, 2007.

[46] U.S. EPA, *Policy Assessment for the Review of the Particulate Matter National Ambient Air Quality Standards*, U.S. EPA Office of Air Quality Planning and Standards, Health and Environmental Impacts Division, EPA 452/R-11-003, April 2011, http://www.epa.gov/ttnnaaqs/standards/pm/data/20110419pmpafinal.pdf.

---

risk assessments, and visibility analyses) of that evidence. **Table B-1** in **Appendix B** provides a chronological listing of EPA's supporting documents leading up to the June 2012 proposed PM NAAQS.

Supplemental to public comments solicited in the *Federal Register*, the CASAC reviewed EPA's drafts and final documents supporting the science and policy behind the Administrator's decisions in the June 2012 PM NAAQS proposal. The CASAC conducted meetings and consultations, and submitted written overviews, providing their views of the validity and completeness of the agency's assessments and findings, and recommending improvements. CASAC's final product, its review of EPA's second external review draft of the "PM Policy Assessment," was completed June 2010.[47]

Table B-2 in **Appendix B** provides a chronological summary of CASAC consultations and reviews of the supporting documents for the June 2012 proposal.

The April 2011 EPA policy assessment ("staff paper") concluded, and the CASAC panel concurred in its final recommendations, that the scientific evidence supported modifying the $PM_{2.5}$ primary standard and considering options for revising the secondary standard for reducing visibility impairment associated with PM. Recognizing certain limitations of the data, the policy assessment included a range of alternatives for consideration by the Administrator for modifying the current PM NAAQS. These recommendations were the core basis for the June 2012 proposal[48] and the Administrator's final decision to revise the PM NAAQS, taking into account other factors including public comments received in response to the June 2012 proposal.

The EPA staff paper included possible modifications to strengthen certain aspects of the PM_{10} standard. However, staff and CASAC placed considerable emphasis on continuing uncertainties and lack of sufficient data to initiate relevant quantitative risk assessment to support such modifications to the standard. As presented in the June 2012 *Federal Register* notice, the Administrator provisionally concluded that the growing evidence continued to support the appropriateness of the existing primary 24-hour PM_{10} standard's protection of short-term health effects, and proposed to retain the existing PM_{10} standard.[49]

A perennial issue in conducting NAAQS reviews is whether the agency is basing its decisions on those studies that reflect the latest science, and that the scientific basis is rigorous and unbiased. In reviewing thousands of studies, the agency staff ultimately needs to establish a cutoff date, or be faced with the need for a continuous review. The current review was based on studies completed by mid-2009, but in the June 29, 2012, *Federal Register* notice EPA indicated that it

---

[47] Until discontinued by the CASAC Chairman in 2005, CASAC historically had signed off in the form of a "closure letter" *only* when the panel of members was convinced that each document accurately reflected the status of the science. The CASAC closure letter was an indication that the majority of the CASAC panel members had generally reached consensus that the criteria documents and the staff paper provided an adequate scientific basis for regulatory decision making. The discontinuance of the closure letter was the subject of considerable debate, particularly within the science community. See CRS Report RL33807, *Air Quality Standards and Sound Science: What Role for CASAC?*, by James E. McCarthy.

[48] See 77 *Federal Register* 38900-38944, *Section III. Rationale for Proposed Decisions on Primary $PM_{2.5}$ Standards*, June 29, 2012.

[49] See 77 *Federal Register* 38944-38963, *Section IV. Rationale for Proposed Decisions on Primary PM_{10} Standards*, June 29, 2012.

is aware that a number of new scientific studies on the health effects of PM have been published since the mid-2009 cutoff date for inclusion in the Integrated Science Assessment. As in the last PM NAAQS review, the EPA intends to conduct a provisional review and assessment of any significant new studies published since the close of the Integrated Science Assessment, including studies that may be submitted during the public comment period on this proposed rule in order to ensure that, before making a final decision, the Administrator is fully aware of the new science that has developed since 2009. In this provisional assessment, the EPA will examine these new studies in light of the literature evaluated in the Integrated Science Assessment. This provisional assessment and a summary of the key conclusions will be placed in the rulemaking docket.[50]

Publication of the proposed PM NAAQS rule in the *Federal Register* on June 29, 2012,[51] started a nine-week public comment period that ran through August 31, 2012. EPA also held two public hearings for the proposal on July 17, 2012, in Philadelphia, PA, and July 19, 2012, in Sacramento, CA.[52] EPA's final determinations for revising the PM NAAQS published on January 15, 2013, were based on information provided in the two public hearings, the more than 230,000 written public comments received, and EPA's consideration of and analysis in response to this information. EPA also revised its Regulatory Impact Analysis (RIA),[53] in large part in response to comments received.

Implementing the Revised PM2.5 NAAQS

Promulgation of NAAQS sets in motion a process under which the states and EPA first identify geographic nonattainment areas, those areas failing to comply with the NAAQS based on monitoring and analysis of relevant air quality data.[54] The CAA is specific with regard to the timelines for determining areas in noncompliance, submission of plans for achieving (or maintaining) compliance, and when noncompliant areas must achieve the established or revised NAAQS.

Within three years of issuance of a NAAQS, states are required to submit "infrastructure" plans demonstrating that they have the basic air quality management components necessary to implement the NAAQS.[55] Following states' proposed and EPA's final designations of attainment and nonattainment areas, states (and tribes if they choose to do so) must submit their plans (State Implementation Plans, or SIPs) for how they will achieve and/or maintain attainment of the

---

[50] See 77 *Federal Register* 38899, *Section II. Background (B) Review of the Air Quality Criteria and Standards for PM (3) Current PM NAAQS Review*, June 29, 2012.

[51] U.S. EPA, National Ambient Air Quality Standards for Particulate Matter, Proposed Rule, 77 *Federal Register* 38889-39055, June 29, 2012. The proposal as signed by EPA Administrator Lisa P. Jackson on June 14, 2012 and supporting documents are available on EPA's website *Particulate Matter (PM): Regulatory Actions*, http://www.epa.gov/pm/actions.html.

[52] U.S. EPA, Public Hearings for Proposed Rules—National Ambient Air Quality Standards for Particulate Matter, 77 *Federal Register* 39205, July 2, 2012.

[53] For key components of the revised RIA see "Important Updates and Analytic Differences Between the PM NAAQS Proposal RIA and the Final RIA," Section ES.5 p. ES-23 of the December 2012 RIA, http://www.epa.gov/pm/2012/finalria.pdf.

[54] For a general overview of the NAAQS designations process, see EPA's "Designations" website at http://www.epa.gov/air/urbanair/designations.html.

[55] Section 110(a)(2) of the Clean Air Act. For a general overview of the NAAQS implementation plans process, see EPA's "State Implementation Plan Overview" website at http://www.epa.gov/air/urbanair/sipstatus/overview.html.

---

standards. These often include new or amended state regulations and new or modified permitting requirements.

If new, or revised, SIPs for attainment establish or revise a transportation-related emissions allowance ("budget"), or add or delete transportation control measures, they will trigger "conformity" determinations. Transportation conformity is required by the CAA, Section 176(c) (42 U.S.C. 7506(c)), to prohibit federal funding and approval for highway and transit projects unless they are consistent with ("conform to") the air quality goals established by a SIP, and will not cause new air quality violations, worsen existing violations, or delay timely attainment of the national ambient air quality standards.[56]

Areas designated nonattainment for the NAAQS also are subject to new source review (NSR) requirements. Enacted as part of the 1977 CAA Amendments and modified in the 1990 CAA Amendments, NSR is designed to ensure that newly constructed facilities, or substantially modified existing facilities, do not result in violation of applicable air quality standards. NSR provisions outline permitting requirements both for construction of new major pollution sources and for modifications to existing major pollution sources.[57] The specific NSR requirements for affected sources depend on whether the sources are subject to "Prevention of Significant Deterioration" (PSD) or nonattainment provisions.[58] As discussed earlier (see "EPA's January 2013 Final Changes to the PM NAAQS"), the January 2013 final PM NAAQS includes revisions to the PSD permitting program (rules) with respect to the revised PM NAAQS so as not to "unreasonably delay" pending permits and establish a "grandfather" provision for permit applications if a draft permit or preliminary determination has been issued for public comment by the date the revised PM NAAQS go into effect.

In addition to the CAA requirement for states to submit implementation plans, EPA acts to control NAAQS pollutants through national regulatory programs. These may be in the form of regulations of products and activities that might emit the pollutants (particularly fuels and combustion engines, such as automobiles and trucks) and in the form of emission standards for new stationary sources (e.g., utilities, refineries). Often these national regulations reflect aspects of state rules previously issued by various states. EPA anticipates that recent CAA rules, including rules to reduce pollution from power plants, clean diesel rules for vehicles, and rules to reduce pollution from stationary diesel engines, would help states meet the revised PM NAAQS.

---

[56] On March 14, 2012, EPA published a final rule restructuring sections of the conformity rule so that existing requirements apply to new or revised NAAQS and released associated implementation guidance July 2012. (U.S. EPA, Office of Transportation and Air Quality, *Guidance for Transportation Conformity Implementation in Multi-Jurisdictional Nonattainment and Maintenance Areas*, July 2012, http://www.epa.gov/otaq/stateresources/transconf/ regs/420b12046.pdf). For transportation conformity regulations see, U.S. EPA "State and Local Transportation Resources: Transportation Conformity" at http://www.epa.gov/otaq/stateresources/transconf/index.htm.

[57] For an overview, including statutory authority and regulations, see EPA's "New Source Review (NSR)" at http://www.epa.gov/air/nsr/.

[58] See Clean Air Act, Part D—Plan Requirements for Nonattainment Areas, sections 171-178, codified at 40 CFR 52.24(f)(10). Section 166 of the CAA authorizes EPA to establish regulations for PSD of any pollutant for which EPA has issued a national standard.

Nonattainment Area Designation Process

The process of designating nonattainment areas is intended as a cooperative federal-state-tribal[59] process in which states and tribes provide initial designation recommendations to EPA for consideration. In Section 107(d)(1)(A) (42 U.S.C. 7407), the statute states that the governor of each state shall submit a list to EPA of all areas in the state, "designating as ... nonattainment, any area that does not meet (*or that contributes to ambient air quality in a nearby area that does not meet*) an air quality standard" (emphasis added). Areas are identified as "attainment/unclassified"[60] when they meet the standard or when the data are insufficient for determining compliance with the NAAQS.

Following state and tribal recommended designation submissions, the EPA Administrator has discretion to make modifications, including to the area boundaries. As required by statute (Section 107(d)1(B)(ii)), the agency must notify the states and tribes regarding any modifications, allowing them sufficient opportunity to demonstrate why a proposed modification is inappropriate, but the final determination rests with EPA.

Measuring and analyzing air quality to determine where NAAQS are not being met is a key step in determining an area's designation. Attainment or nonattainment designations are made primarily on the basis of three years of federally referenced monitoring data.[61] EPA began developing methods for monitoring fine particles at the time the $PM_{2.5}$ NAAQS were being finalized in 1997, and operation of the network of monitors for $PM_{2.5}$ was phased in from 1999 through 2000. The network of monitors and their locations have been modified over time. Most recently, in a separate action in conjunction with the October 2006 publication of the revised particulates NAAQS, EPA amended its national air quality monitoring requirements, including those for monitoring particle pollution.[62] The amended monitoring requirements were intended to help federal, state, and local air quality agencies by adopting improvements in monitoring technology. Additional modifications to the PM NAAQS monitoring network were included in the final January 2013 rule, as discussed earlier in this report.

In addition to air emission and air quality data, EPA considers a number of other relevant factors when designating nonattainment areas,[63] and recommends that states apply these factors in their determinations in conjunction with other technical guidance. Examples of these factors include population density and degree of urbanization (including commercial development), growth rates, traffic and commuting patterns, weather and transport patterns, and geography/topography. States

---

[59] Though not required, tribes have been encouraged to submit recommendations. The area designation requirements under the CAA (Section 107) are specific with respect to states, but not to tribes. EPA follows the same designation process for tribes per Sections 110(o) and 301(d) of the CAA and pursuant to the 1988 Tribal Authority Rule, which specifies that tribes shall be treated as states in selected cases (40 CFR Part 49). For information regarding tribes that have participated in the $PM_{2.5}$ designation recommendation process, see http://www.epa.gov/pmdesignations.

[60] Section 107(d)(1)(A)(iii) of the CAA provides that any area that EPA cannot designate on the basis of available information as meeting or not meeting the standards should be designated unclassifiable.

[61] A federally referenced monitor is one that has been accepted for use by EPA for comparison of the NAAQS by meeting the design specifications and certain precision and bias (performance) specifications (40 CFR Part 58).

[62] Revisions to Ambient Air Monitoring Regulations, final rule, 71 *Federal Register* 61235-61328, October 17, 2006. http://www.epa.gov/air/particlepollution/actions.html.

[63] See Chapter 5 of the EPA Technical Support Document for December 17, 2004, final designations for the 1997 $PM_{2.5}$ NAAQS and April 2005 modifications, for explanations of these factors; available at http://www.epa.gov/pmdesignations/1997standards/tech.htm.

---

and tribes may submit additional information on factors they believe are relevant for EPA to consider.

Nonattainment areas include those counties where pollutant concentrations exceed the standard as well as those that contribute to exceedance of the standard in adjoining counties. Entire metropolitan areas tend to be designated nonattainment, even if only one county in the area has readings worse than the standard. In addition to identifying whether monitored violations are occurring, states' or tribes' boundary recommendations for an area are to also show that violations are not occurring in those portions of the recommended area that have been excluded, and that they do not contain emission sources that contribute to the observed violations.

January 2013 Final Revised PM₂.₅ Annual NAAQS: Potential Area Designations

The January 2013 final rule revising the $PM_{2.5}$ annual standard is expected to result in an increase in the number of areas (typically defined by counties or portions of counties) designated nonattainment. Similar to the revisions to the $PM_{2.5}$ daily (24-hour) standard in 2006, the January 2013 revised concentrations for the $PM_{2.5}$ annual standard are expected to affect primarily areas currently in nonattainment for the 2006 standards, but would also likely include a few counties that have not been previously designated as nonattainment. EPA would not require new nonattainment designations for PM_{10} primary NAAQS since the standards were not changed in the January 2013 final rule.

The effective date of final PM NAAQS revisions corresponds with the January 15, 2013, publication in the *Federal Register*. State and tribal area designation recommendations would be required under the CAA to be submitted to EPA by January 2014 (within one year of the effective date of the final rule). The CAA requires EPA to make its final area designations within one year of the state and tribal recommendations, projected to be January 2015. EPA is required to notify states and tribes of its intended modifications to their recommendations 120 days (projected to be August-September 2014) prior to promulgating final designations which are expected to become effective sometime in early 2015.

The actual area designations of nonattainment are more than two years away and will be based on more current monitoring data (likely 2011-2013) and several other factors. Based on anticipated reductions associated with several other existing national air pollution control regulations and programs (see discussion in "National Regulations" section), EPA predicted that seven counties in California would be the only areas unable to meet the new $PM_{2.5}$ primary standard by 2020.[64] Additionally, for illustrative purposes, EPA identified 66 counties with monitors that show concentrations of $PM_{2.5}$ that would exceed the revised limit of the primary annual standard of 12 $\mu g/m^3$ based on 2009-2011 air quality monitoring data.[65] According to EPA, 47 of these counties were determined nonattainment areas previously for $PM_{2.5}$ NAAQS based on earlier monitoring data available at the time and other factors considered.

---

[64] See list of counties (http://www.epa.gov/pm/2012/2020table.pdfand) and map (http://www.epa.gov/pm/2012/2020map.pdf) depicting EPA's predictions for 2020, available on EPA's website *Particulate Matter (PM): Regulatory Actions*, http://www.epa.gov/pm/actions.html.

[65] At the time of the June 2012 proposal, EPA had identified counties with monitors that showed concentrations of $PM_{2.5}$ that would exceed the proposed revised range of the primary annual standard of 12 $\mu g/m^3$ to 13 $\mu g/m^3$ based on 2008-2010 monitoring data.

The map in **Figure 1** below depicts the potential nonattainment areas (counties) for the revised PM$_{2.5}$ annual standards based solely on the 2009-2011 air quality monitoring. The areas are depicted in the map for illustration purposes as a rough approximation of the potential areas that may be designated nonattainment, as they do not take into account other factors generally considered in making final designation determinations. The specific counties based on the 2009-2011 monitoring data are shown in **Appendix C**, which also shows the overlap of those nonattainment areas for the existing (2006) PM$_{2.5}$ annual and/or daily (24-hour) standards, and indicates those areas not previously designated nonattainment. An apt direct comparison of areas expected to be designated nonattainment for the final 2013 revised PM$_{2.5}$ standards based solely on monitoring data with *all* areas designated nonattainment (counties and portions of counties) for the prior (2006 and 1997) PM NAAQS[66] is not practical, since some counties may have been determined attainment or nonattainment at that time based on consideration of factors in addition to relevant monitoring. Overlaying those counties with monitors identified by EPA based only on 2009-2011 monitoring data provides some indication of potential areas that may be considered for nonattainment designations. EPA expects data from future monitoring, 2011-2013, will possibly show continued decline in levels of PM and their precursors, resulting in fewer nonattainment areas than shown by the 66 counties approximated.

---

[66] For additional information, see CRS Report R40096, *2006 National Ambient Air Quality Standards (NAAQS) for Fine Particulate Matter (PM2.5): Designating Nonattainment Areas*, by Robert Esworthy.

Figure 1. Counties Not Meeting the January 2013 Revised Primary Annual PM$_{2.5}$ NAAQS Based on 2009-2011 Air Monitoring Data

(revised annual standard of 12 µg/m³)

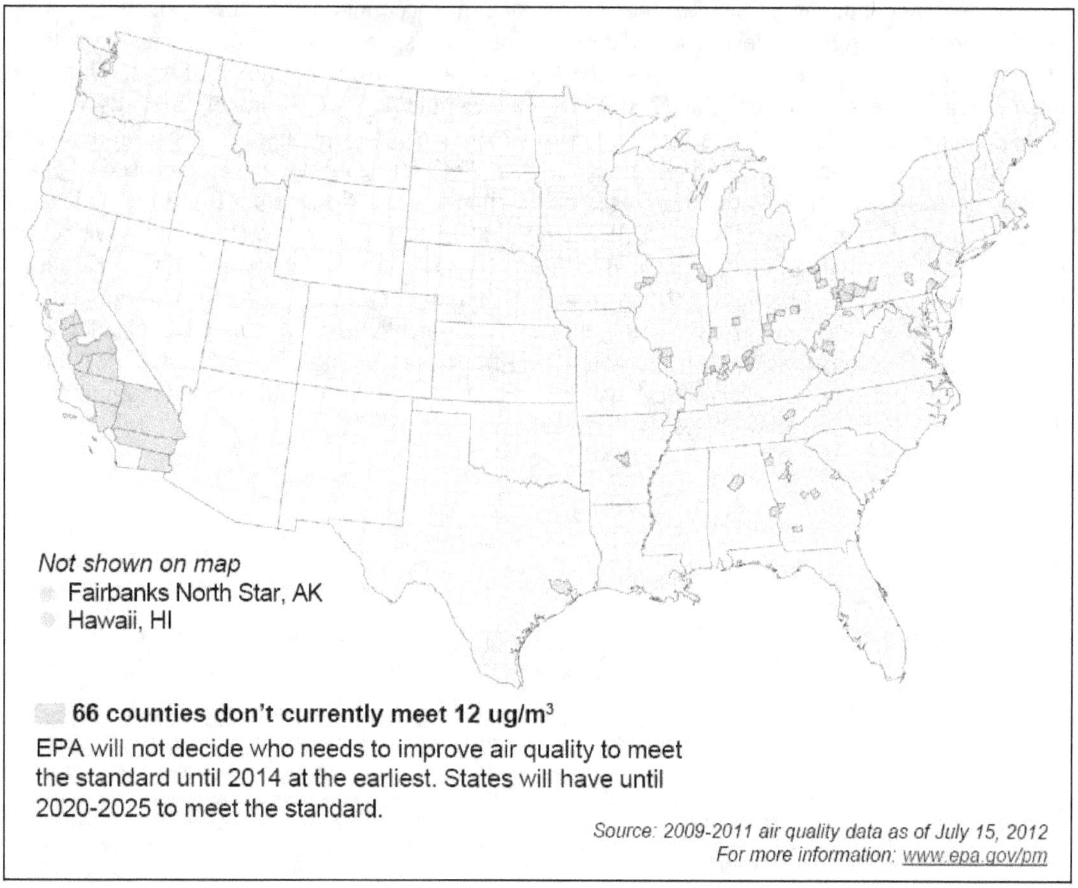

Not shown on map
  Fairbanks North Star, AK
  Hawaii, HI

■ **66 counties don't currently meet 12 ug/m³**
EPA will not decide who needs to improve air quality to meet the standard until 2014 at the earliest. States will have until 2020-2025 to meet the standard.

Source: 2009-2011 air quality data as of July 15, 2012
For more information: www.epa.gov/pm

Source: U.S. EPA, http://www.epa.gov/pm/2012/mapb.pdf. The above map, other maps and supporting documents regarding the January 2013 PM$_{2.5}$ NAAQS revisions are available on EPA's website *Particulate Matter (PM): Regulatory Actions*, http://www.epa.gov/pm/actions.html.

Notes: Forty-seven of the counties shown were nonattainment areas previously for PM$_{2.5}$ NAAQS. Specific counties are shown in **Appendix C**. The designations are presented for illustrative purposes only. EPA will not designate areas as nonattainment for the revised PM$_{2.5}$ NAAQS based on 2009-2011 air monitoring data. Designations will most likely be based on 2011-2013 air monitoring data that the agency anticipates will indicate comparatively improved air quality.

The 2006 revisions to the PM NAAQS tightening the 24-hour standard, which are currently being implemented, primarily affected urban areas. EPA published its final designations of 31 areas in 18 states, comprising 120 counties (89 counties and portions of 31 additional counties) for nonattainment of the revised 2006 *24-hour* $PM_{2.5}$ standard, on November 13, 2009.[67] Based on the 2009-2011 data, 28 of the 120 counties designated nonattainment for the 2006 PM 24-hour standard would be in nonattainment for the January 2013 annual standard. The designations, based on 2006 through 2008 air quality monitoring data, included a few counties that were designated nonattainment for $PM_{2.5}$ for the first time, but the majority of the counties identified overlapped with EPA's final nonattainment designations for the 1997 $PM_{2.5}$ NAAQS.[68] It is important to note that most of the 1997 $PM_{2.5}$ nonattainment areas were *only* exceeding the annual standard; thus, tightening the 24-hour standard resulted in an increased number of areas being designated nonattainment based on exceedances of both the 24-hour *and* the annual standard. The majority of the roughly 3,000 counties throughout the United States (including tribal lands) were designated attainment/unclassifiable, and are not required to impose additional emission control measures to reduce $PM_{2.5}$.

State Implementation Plans (SIPs)

The CAA requires that within three years of issuance of a NAAQS, states are required to submit "infrastructure" plans demonstrating that they have the basic air quality management components necessary to implement the NAAQS.[69] Areas designated attainment/unclassifiable will not have to take steps to improve air quality, but under the statute they must take steps to prevent air quality from deteriorating to unhealthy levels ("maintenance plans"). For those areas eventually designated nonattainment, state, local, and tribal governments must outline detailed control requirements in plans demonstrating how they will meet the revised primary annual $PM_{2.5}$ NAAQS.

These plans, defined as state implementation plans and referred to as SIPs (TIPs for tribal implementation plans), must be submitted to EPA three years after the effective date of the agency's final designations.[70] EPA projects final area designations will be effective early 2015 for the January 2013 PM NAAQS revisions, thus SIPs and TIPs would be required by early 2018. If states fail to develop an adequate implementation plan, EPA can impose one. Under the CAA, states are required to meet any established or revised $PM_{2.5}$ standard "as expeditiously as practicable," but no later than five years from the effective date of designation—December 2020 according to EPA's timeline—unless an extension (up to five additional years) allowed under the CAA is granted.[71] Changes in pollution control measures by affected sources (e.g., industrial

---

[67] 74 *Federal Register* 58688-58781, November 13, 2009; see also "Area Designations for 2006 24-Hour Fine Particulate ($PM_{2.5}$) Standards—Regulatory Actions," http://www.epa.gov/pmdesignations/2006standards/regs.htm#4. Publication of a final area designation rule for the 2006 24-hour $PM_{2.5}$ NAAQS had been delayed as a result of the incoming Administration's review of the final rule, along with several other agency proposed and final actions introduced toward the end of the previous Administration. See footnote 66.

[68] For detailed $PM_{2.5}$ state/county geographical designation recommendations by EPA and those from individual states and tribes, for the 1997 and for the 2006 $PM_{2.5}$ NAAQS, see http://www.epa.gov/pmdesignations.

[69] Section 110(a)(2) of the Clean Air Act. For a general overview of the NAAQS implementation plans process, see EPA's "State Implementation Plan Overview" at http://www.epa.gov/air/urbanair/sipstatus/overview.html.

[70] Section 172 of the Clean Air Act. See EPA's "State Implementation Plan Overview" at http://www.epa.gov/air/urbanair/sipstatus/overview.html.

[71] Under Section 172(a)(2)(A) of the CAA, EPA may grant an area an extension of the initial attainment date for one to five years (in no case later than 10 years after the designation date for the area). A state requesting an extension must (continued...)

---

operations, power plants, etc.) would not be required as a result of NAAQS revisions until after the area designations (see discussion in previous sections) are finalized or after the SIPs are finalized, depending on the specific circumstances.

National Regulations

EPA anticipates that in many cases, stationary and mobile source controls and additional reductions currently being adopted to attain the 2006 $PM_{2.5}$ standards in conjunction with expected emission reductions from implementing national regulations and strategies will help states meet the proposed standards. These national actions EPA referenced include the

- Cross-State Air Pollution Rule (CSAPR);[72]

- Mercury and Air Toxics Standards (MATS);[73]

- Light-Duty Vehicle Tier 2 Rule;[74]

- Heavy Duty Diesel Rule;[75]

- Clean Air Nonroad Diesel Rule;[76]

- Regional Haze Regulations and Guidelines for Best Available Retrofit Technology Determinations;[77]

- NOx Emission Standard for New Commercial Aircraft Engines;[78]

- Emissions Standards for Locomotives and Marine Compression-Ignition Engines;[79]

- Control of Emissions from Nonroad Spark Ignition Engines and Equipment;[80]

- Category 3 Oceangoing Vessels;[81]

(...continued)

submit an implementation plan (SIP) by the required deadline that includes, among other things, sufficient information demonstrating that attainment by the initial attainment date is "impracticable."

[72] 76 *Federal Register* 48208-48483, August 8, 2011. The CSPAR was intended to replace EPA's 2005 Clean Air Interstate Rule (CAIR, 70 *Federal Register* 25162, May 12, 2005), promulgated under the CAA, 42 U.S.C. 7401 et seq.; see http://www.epa.gov/crossstaterule/index.html. The CAIR had been remanded by the D.C. Circuit and to EPA in 2008 (North Carolina v. EPA 531 F.3d 896 (D.C. Cir. 2008)). For information regarding the CAIR rule see CRS Report RL34589, *Clean Air After the CAIR Decision: Multi-Pollutant Approaches to Controlling Powerplant Emissions*, by James E. McCarthy, Larry Parker, and Robert Meltz, and EPA "Clean Air Interstate Rule" at http://www.epa.gov/air/interstateairquality/#older.

[73] 77 *Federal Register* 9304-9513, February 16, 2012.

[74] 65 *Federal Register* 6822-6870, February 10, 2000.

[75] 65 *Federal Register* 59896-59978, October 6, 2000.

[76] 69 *Federal Register* 38958-39273, January 29, 2004.

[77] 70 *Federal Register* 39104-39172, July 6, 2005.

[78] 70 *Federal Register* 69644-69687, November 17, 2005.

[79] 73 *Federal Register* 37095-37144, republished June 30, 2008.

[80] 73 *Federal Register* 59034-59380, October 8, 2008.

[81] 75 *Federal Register* 22896-23065, April 30, 2010.

- Reciprocating Internal Combustion Engines (RICE) National Emissions Standards for Hazardous Air Pollutants (NESHAPS);[82] and

- New Source Performance Standards and Emissions Guidelines for Hospital/Medical/Infectious Waste Incinerators Final Rule Amendments.[83]

Stakeholders and some Members of Congress are skeptical about EPA's expectations with respect to the corollary benefits associated with some of these regulations, and raise concerns about pending efforts to delay some of the more recent programs and historical delays of others. Of particular concern are the Cross-State Air Pollution Rule ("Cross-State Rule," or CSAPR),[84] which was to have gone into effect in 2012 but was stayed in December 2011, then vacated on August 21, 2012, by the D.C. Circuit Court of Appeals,[85] and the Mercury and Air Toxics Standards (MATS), which EPA itself has stayed with regard to new plants, pending reconsideration. On October 5, 2012, the U.S. Department of Justice filed a petition[86] seeking en banc rehearing of the D.C. Circuit's August 21, 2012, decision regarding the CSAPR. Other rules remanded or reconsidered include the hazardous air pollutant ("MACT") standards for boilers and cement kilns. EPA has delayed implementation of the boiler MACT rules for more than a year and a half while considering changes to the requirements. The agency has also extended the compliance deadline for the cement kiln MACT by two years.

Potential Impacts of More Stringent PM Standards

The impacts of the revising PM NAAQS can be both potentially far-reaching and indirect. As discussed earlier in this report, the NAAQS by itself does not compel any specific direct pollution control measures. Rather it starts a process that could result in significant required investments by emitting sources in control measures. In addition to these costs, the eventual result is projected by EPA to be potentially significant health benefits. Estimates of health and welfare risk reductions and costs associated with control strategies for areas potentially not in compliance provide some insights into potential impacts of the June 2012 proposed and January 2013 final revisions to the PM NAAQS.

The Clean Air Act requires that NAAQS be set solely on the basis of public health and welfare protection, while costs and feasibility are generally taken into account in implementation of the NAAQS (a process that is primarily a state responsibility). As discussed previously, in setting and revising the NAAQS, the CAA directs the EPA Administrator to protect public health *with an*

---

[82] 75 *Federal Register* 51570-51608, August 20, 2010; Proposed Amendments 77 *Federal Register* 33812-33857, June 7, 2012.

[83] 74 *Federal Register* 51415, October 6, 2009.

[84] See U.S. EPA, "Federal Implementation Plans: Interstate Transport of Fine Particulate Matter and Ozone and Correction of SIP Approvals," 76 *Federal Register* 48208-48483, August 8, 2011, http://www.gpo.gov/fdsys/pkg/FR-2011-08-08/pdf/2011-17600.pdf. Explanatory and background material can be found on EPA's website at http://www.epa.gov/crossstaterule/actions.html. See also footnote 72.

[85] *EME Homer City Generation, L.P. v. Environmental Protection Agency*, D.C. Cir., No. 11-1302, August 21, 2012, http://www.cadc.uscourts.gov/internet/opinions.nsf/19346B280C78405C85257A61004DC0E5/$file/11-1302-1390314.pdf. See also U.S. EPA's website, "Cross-State Air Pollution Rule (CSAPR)," http://epa.gov/crossstaterule/ for this decision and other related documents.

[86] U.S. EPA, http://epa.gov/crossstaterule/pdfs/Rehearing_Petition_617874.pdf. For status of the petition see EPA website, "Cross-State Air Pollution Rule (CSAPR)," at http://epa.gov/crossstaterule/.

---

adequate margin of safety. This language has been interpreted, both by the agency and by the courts, as requiring standards be based on a review of the health impacts, without consideration of the costs, technological feasibility, or other non-health criteria.[87]

Nevertheless, coinciding with the PM NAAQS final rule released on December 14, 2012, and proposed rule in the June 29, 2012, *Federal Register*, EPA released regulatory impact analyses (RIA)[88] assessing the costs and benefits of setting the standard at the proposed and other alternative levels, to meet its obligations under Executive Order 12866 and in compliance with guidance from the White House Office of Management and Budget.[89] EPA emphasized that the RIA is for informational purposes and that decisions regarding revisions to the PM NAAQS are not based on consideration of the analyses in the RIA in any way. In addition, the expected costs are more difficult to predict than for many other regulations because the ultimate pollution control requirements, which are the primary costs, will depend on a variety of factors, such as state regulatory decisions and the results of monitoring and modeling analysis of designated areas that are not fully knowable at this time.

In part in response to comments received and considered following the June 2012 proposal, EPA revised its RIA for the final rule.[90] **Table 2** below presents a range of EPA's estimated economic costs, monetized benefits, and net benefits (subtracting total costs from the monetized benefits) associated with achieving the revised PM$_{2.5}$ standards in the final rule published in January 2013, and other alternatives considered as presented in EPA's revised RIA.

---

[87] With regard to the non-relevance of cost considerations, see generally Whitman v. American Trucking Associations, 531 U.S. 457, 465-472, 475-76 (2001).

[88] U.S. EPA, "*Regulatory Impact Analysis for the Final Revisions to the National Ambient Air Quality Standards for Particulate Matter*," http://www.epa.gov/pm/2012/finalria.pdf, and U.S. EPA, "Regulatory Impact Analysis for the Proposed Revisions to the National Ambient Air Quality Standards for Particulate Matter," EPA-452/R-12-003 June 2012, available at http://www.epa.gov/ttn/ecas/ria.html.

[89] 58 *Federal Register* 51735, October 4, 1993. See the White House OMB website, *Regulatory Matters*, at http://www.whitehouse.gov/omb/regulatory_affairs/default.

[90] See footnote 53.

Table 2. EPA's Estimated Total Monetized Benefits, Costs, and Net Benefits of Attaining Alternative PM₂.₅ NAAQS as in 2020 for the January 2013 Final Rule

(2010 $ in millions)

Final and Alternative Annual Standard (μg/m³)	Estimated Monetized Benefits[a]		Estimated Total Costs[b]	Estimated Net Benefits	
	Discount Rate[c]				
	3%	7%	7%	3%	7%
13	$1,300 to $2,900		$11 to $100	$1,200 to $2,900	$1,100 to $2,600
12	$4,000 to $9,100	$3,600 to $8,200	$53 to $350	$3,700 to $9,000	$3,300 to $8,100
11	$13,000 to $29,000	$12,000 to $26,000	$320 to $1,700	$11,000 to $29,000	$10,000 to $26,000

Source: Adapted from Environmental Protection Agency's "U.S. EPA, "Regulatory Impact Analysis for the Final Revisions to the National Ambient Air Quality Standards for Particulate Matter," December 2012, Table ES-2, p. ES-15, http://www.epa.gov/pm/2012/finalria.pdf. Estimates and results are as reported by EPA and have been rounded after calculation.

Note: Results are rounded to two significant digits after calculation for presentation and computation as reported by EPA. Estimates (costs and benefits) reflect full attainment in 2020, which includes implementation of several national programs and are incremental to compliance with the 2006 PM₂.₅ NAAQS. The discount rates are as recommended in EPA's *Guidelines for Preparing Economic Analyses (2000)* and OMB Circular A-4 (2003).

a. The reduction in premature deaths each year accounts for over 90% of total monetized benefits. Mortality risk evaluation assumes discounting over the Science Advisory Board-recommended 20-year segmented lag structure. Not all possible benefits or "disbenefits" are quantified and monetized in this analysis. Data limitations prevented EPA from quantifying these endpoints, and as such, these benefits are inherently more uncertain than those benefits that EPA was able to quantify.

b. The two cost estimates do not represent lower- and upper-bound estimates, but represent estimates generated by two different methodologies. The lower estimate is generated using the fixed-cost methodology, which assumes that technological change and innovation will result in the availability of additional controls by 2020 that are similar in cost to the higher end of the cost range for current, known controls. The higher estimate is generated using the hybrid methodology, which assumes that while additional controls may become available by 2020, they become available at an increasing cost, and the increasing cost varies by geographic area and by degree of difficulty associated with obtaining the needed emissions reductions.

c. Due to data limitations, EPA was unable to discount compliance costs for all sectors at the 3% discount rate. Consequently, the net benefit calculations at 3% were computed by subtracting the costs at the 7% rate from the monetized benefits with the 3% rate.

As shown in **Table 2**, EPA estimated that the monetized benefits associated with the January 2013 final revised PM₂.₅ annual standard of 12 μg/m³ would range $4.0 billion to $9.1 billion per year in 2020 (2010 $), compared to annual costs ranging from $53.0 million to $350.0 million. EPA also noted that a full accounting of benefits would include additional environmental and societal benefits that were not quantified in the analysis. The basis for the benefits calculations[91] are health and welfare impacts attributable to reductions in ambient concentration of PM₂.₅ resulting from a reasonable, but "speculative," array of known state implementation emission control strategies selected by EPA for purposes of analysis. The analysis does not model the specific

---

[91] See p. Section ES.2.2. beginning on p. ES-10, and discussion of health benefits in Chapter 5 beginning p. 5-1, and welfare benefits in Chapter 6 p. 6-1 of the EPA December 2012 RIA, footnote 88.

actions that each state will undertake or emerging technologies in implementing the alternative $PM_{2.5}$ NAAQS. EPA notes that reductions in annual premature deaths represent a substantial proportion of total monetized benefits (over 90%).[92]

EPA estimated total costs under partial and full attainment of several alternative PM standards.[93] The engineering costs generally include the costs of purchasing, installing, and operating the referenced control technologies. The technologies and control strategies selected for analysis are illustrative of one way in which nonattainment areas could meet a revised standard. EPA anticipates that in actual SIPS, state and local governments will consider programs that are best suited for local conditions as there are various options for potential control programs that would bring areas into attainment with alternative standards. EPA includes a detailed discussion of the limitations and uncertainties associated with the benefits assumptions and analyses.[94]

While recognizing the need to adequately protect against potential health concerns associated with PM, some Members and stakeholders are apprehensive that EPA has underestimated potential costs and are concerned with the potential monetary consequences associated given the current economic environment. In particular, some stakeholders question the validity of EPA's reliance on the associated impacts of other national regulations in reducing the potential burdens. Critics are concerned that this results in underestimating the number of areas (counties) likely to be affected in terms of their ability to attain the proposed alternative PM NAAQS and the expected associated costs of necessary measures that will be required in the form of SIPs.

Reaction to the Revised PM NAAQS

Prior to EPA's June 2012 proposed rule to revise the PM NAAQS, stakeholders were providing evidence and arguments in letters, press releases, at public hearings and other forums for their preferred recommendations, and EPA received numerous comments during various stages of development of the criteria and policy documents. In general, business and industry opposed more stringent standards particularly in light of the current national and global economic environment; and public health and environmental advocacy groups advocated support for more stringent standards based on the continuing evidence of health effects from ongoing scientific research. As mentioned earlier, several states petitioned EPA, and subsequently filed suit in the D.C. Circuit Court urging timely completion of EPA's review of the PM NAAQS in response to the February 2009 remand. Other state air quality regulators recognized the need to ensure adequate health protection from PM, but expressed concerns about the impacts of more stringent PM NAAQS on already strained state budgets.

Proponents of more stringent standards generally stress that

- the $PM_{2.5}$ standards should be at least as stringent as the more stringent combined daily and annual levels recommended in the 2006 EPA staff paper, and those recommended by the CASAC;

---

[92] U.S. EPA, p. ES-15 December 2012 RIA; see footnote 88.

[93] See discussion for engineering cost analysis in Chapter 7 beginning p. 7-1 (pdf p. 455) June 2012 RIA, footnote 88.

[94] See the Executive Summary in the RIA accompanying the January 2013 final rule: ES.4 Caveats and Limitations, beginning on p. ES-21.

- scientific evidence of adverse health effects is more compelling than when the standards were revised in 2006;

- more stringent standards ensure continued progress toward protection of public health with an adequate margin of safety as required by the CAA;

- welfare effects, particularly visibility, should be enhanced.

Critics of more stringent PM NAAQS stress that

- more stringent (and in some cases the existing) standards are not justified by the scientific evidence; the proposal does not take into account studies completed since the 2009 cutoff;

- requiring the same level of stringency for all fine particles without distinguishing sources is unfounded;

- costs and adverse impacts on regions and sectors of the economy are excessive;

- EPA has potentially overstated the expected benefits and underestimated expected costs;

- revising the standards could impede implementation of the existing (2006) PM NAAQS and the process of bringing areas into compliance, given the current status of this process;

- the benefits (and costs) associated with implementation of the 2006 PM NAAQS, as well as compliance with other relatively recent EPA air quality regulations that are being implemented, have not yet been realized;

- revisions to PM NAAQS are unnecessary as shown by EPA's trends data that annual and 24-hour measured PM national concentrations have declined 24% and 28% respectively from 2001 to 2010.

Congressional Activity

Not long after EPA's release of its PM NAAQS proposal, the House Committee on Energy and Commerce Subcommittee on Energy and Power held a hearing on June 28, 2012,[95] on the potential impacts of tightening the $PM_{2.5}$ NAAQS. The focus of the debate was the regulatory costs and burdens associated with the implementation of the revised standards, and potential impacts on economic growth, employment and consumers. Just prior to EPA's release of the June 2012 proposal, several Members urged the Administrator to include retaining the current (as of 2006) $PM_{2.5}$ standard as an option for consideration in the agency's proposal.[96] In November 2012, some Members[97] urged EPA to consider delaying the final rule, while conversely, others,

---

[95] House Committee on Energy and Commerce Subcommittee on Energy and Power June 28, 2012 hearing entitled, "The American Energy Initiative: A Focus on the New Proposal to Tighten National Standards for Fine Particulate Matter," http://energycommerce.house.gov/hearing/american-energy-initiative-focus-new-proposal-tighten-national-standards-fine-particulate.

[96] See joint letter from Representatives Fred Upton, Chairman, Committee on Energy and Commerce, Ed Whitfield, Chairman, Subcommittee on Energy and Power, and Joe Barton, Chairman Emeritus, June 6, 2012, http://energycommerce.house.gov/letter/letter-epa-regarding-national-ambient-air-quality-standards.

[97] See November 21, 2012, letter from 47 Members of the House of Representatives to the U.S. EPA Administrator, (continued...)

along with some state attorneys general,[98] supported timely completion of the agency's review. As mentioned earlier in this report, also in November 2012, some Members recommended EPA reconsider its calculations of costs and benefits supporting the proposed rule. Also, although the January 15, 2013, final rule did not modify the standards for inhalable "coarse" particles larger than 2.5 but smaller than 10 microns (PM_{10}), nor were modifications proposed in June 2012, some Members maintained a particular interest in EPA's consideration of the PM_{10} standards.

During the second session of the 111th and during the first session of the 112th Congress, some Members raised concerns in letters to the EPA Administrator and during oversight hearings[99] about EPA's staff draft reports and CASAC recommendations regarding changes to the PM NAAQS leading up to the June 2012 proposal. Some Members expressed their concerns of potential impacts that the options for changing PM NAAQS standards could have on industry and on agricultural operations. In letters to the EPA Administrator, several Members also communicated their particular concerns with the agency's consideration of stricter standards for coarse particulates (PM_{10}), including apprehensions of how changes may affect the agricultural community.[100] Additionally, during the 112th Congress, the House-passed Farm Dust Regulation Prevention Act of 2011 (H.R. 1633) would have prohibited EPA from proposing, finalizing, implementing, or enforcing any regulation revising primary or secondary NAAQS applicable to PM "... with an aerodynamic diameter greater than 2.5 micrometers ..." for one year. Further, the House-passed bill would have amended the CAA to exempt "nuisance dust" from the act and would have excluded nuisance dust from references in the act to particulate matter "... except with respect to geographic areas where such dust is not regulated under state, tribal, or local law.... " Nuisance dust was defined in the bill as particulate matter that

> (1) is generated primarily from natural sources, unpaved roads, agricultural activities, earth moving, or other activities typically conducted in rural areas; (2) consists primarily of soil, other natural or biological materials, windblown dust, or some combination thereof; (3) is not emitted directly into the ambient air from combustion, such as exhaust from combustion engines and emissions from stationary combustion processes; (4) is not comprised of residuals from the combustion of coal; and (5) does not include radioactive particulate matter produced from uranium mining or processing.

(...continued)

http://latta.house.gov/uploadedfiles/2012_11_29_final_pm2_5_letter_signed_w_attchmt.pdf. Also see press release available on Representative Bob Latta's website at http://latta.house.gov/news/documentsingle.aspx?DocumentID= 314585.

[98] See December 6, 2012, letter from nine State Attorneys General to the Acting Administrator of the Office of Information and Regulatory Affairs, the White House Office of Management and Budget, http://www.eenews.net/assets/2012/12/10/document_gw_02.pdf.

[99] For example, U.S. Congress, Senate Committee on Agriculture, Nutrition, and Forestry, *Oversight Hearing to Examine the Impact of EPA Regulation on Agriculture*, 111th Cong., 2nd sess., September 23, 2010; and U.S. Congress, House Committee on Agriculture, *Public Hearing to Review the Impact of EPA Regulation on Agriculture*, 112th Cong., 1st sess., March 10, 2011.

[100] Examples of letters to EPA Administrator Lisa Jackson include, but are not limited to, a joint letter from 99 House Members, March 29, 2011, http://fincher.house.gov/press-release/fincher-noem-call-epa-abandon-unreasonable-dust-standards; a joint letter from 75 House Members, September 27, 2010, http://agriculture.house.gov/letter/letter-epa-national-ambient-air-quality-standards-naaqs-particulate-matter-dust; a joint letter from 21 Senators, July 23, 2010, http://grassley.senate.gov/about/upload/Agriculture-07-23-10-dust-letter-to-EPA-signed-version-doc.pdf; an August 5, 2010, joint letter from former Senators Kent Conrad and Byron Dorgan and former Representative Earl Pomeroy. See also CRS Report R41622, *Environmental Regulation and Agriculture*, coordinated by Megan Stubbs.

A general provision included in FY2012 House-reported EPA appropriations language (H.R. 2584, Title IV, and §454)[101] would have restricted the use of FY2012 appropriations "to modify the national primary ambient air quality standard or the national secondary ambient air quality standard applicable to coarse particulate matter (generally referred to as "PM_{10}")."[102] No comparable provision was retained in the Consolidated Appropriations Act, 2012 (P.L. 112-74), enacted December 23, 2011, which ultimately included EPA's FY2012 appropriation.

NAAQS decisions have often been a source of significant concern to many in Congress. The evolution and development of the PM (and ozone) NAAQS, in particular, have been the subject of extensive oversight. For example, following promulgations of the 1997 NAAQS Congress held 28 days of hearings on the EPA rule. Congress enacted legislation specifying deadlines for implementation of the 1997 standard, funding for monitoring and research of potential health effects, and the coordination of the PM (and ozone) standard with other air quality regulations. During the 109th Congress, hearings were held regarding implementation and review of the PM NAAQS leading up to promulgations of the 2006 PM NAAQS.[103]

Because of the potential impacts PM NAAQS could have on both public health and the economy, EPA's final rule published on January 15, 2013, modifying these standards has generated mixed reactions from some Members, and the issue will likely be of continued interest in the 113th Congress.

Conclusions

EPA's changes to the PM NAAQS in its final rule published on January 15, 2013, following completion of its statutorily required review, have continued to garner attention and conflicting concerns among a diverse array of stakeholders, and in Congress. As evidenced by the history of the PM NAAQS, the level of scrutiny and oversight could increase in the coming months. Because both the health and economic consequences of particulate matter standards are potentially significant, the PM NAAQS are likely to remain a prominent issue in the 113th Congress.

EPA asserts that its review and analyses of scientific evidence showed that revising the PM NAAQS could potentially result in fewer adverse health effects for the general population and particularly sensitive populations such as children, asthmatics, and the elderly, as well as improved welfare effects. Nonetheless, concerns remain with regard to the potential associated costs. In its assessment of the impacts of revising the PM NAAQS, EPA expects relatively few additional areas (counties) will be in nonattainment and require more stringent pollution controls to achieve compliance. Industry, some Members and some state representatives anticipate that the January 2013 revised PM NAAQS could result in more areas than anticipated by EPA being

---

[101] The Department of the Interior, Environment, and Related Agencies Appropriations Act, 2012 (H.R. 2584, Title IV Section 454) as reported by the House Committee on Appropriations on July 19, 2011. From July 25, 2011, to July 28, 2011, the House considered H.R. 2584 as reported July 19, 2011, but the House floor debate was suspended.

[102] See CRS Report R42332, *Environmental Protection Agency (EPA) FY2012 Appropriations*, by Robert Esworthy, and CRS Report R41979, *Environmental Protection Agency (EPA) FY2012 Appropriations: Overview of Provisions in H.R. 2584 as Reported*, by Robert Esworthy.

[103] For example, see U.S. Senate Committee on Environment and Public Works, Subcommittee on Clean Air, Climate Change, and Nuclear Safety, *Implementation of the Existing Particulate Matter and Ozone Air Quality Standards*, November 10, 2005.

classified as nonattainment and needing to implement new controls on particulate matter. Further, they are concerned that stricter standards may mean more costs for the transportation and industrial sectors, including utilities, refineries, and the trucking industry, affected by particulate matter controls. Others stress that related ongoing control efforts from prior and recently promulgated actions are expected to reduce the potential number of nonattainment areas, or at least facilitate compliance.

EPA's review and establishment of the 1997 PM NAAQS was the subject of litigation and challenges, including a Supreme Court decision in 2001.[104] EPA's 1997 promulgation of standards for both coarse and fine particulate matter prompted critics to charge EPA with over-regulation and spurred environmental groups to claim that EPA had not gone far enough. Not only was the science behind the PM NAAQS challenged, but EPA was also accused of unconstitutional behavior. More than 100 plaintiffs sued to overturn the standard. Although EPA's decision to issue the standards was upheld unanimously by the Supreme Court, for the most part, stakeholders on both sides of the issue continued to advocate their recommendations for more stringent and less stringent PM standard. Several states and industry, agriculture, business, and environmental and public health advocacy groups petitioned the U.S. Court of Appeals for the District of Columbia Circuit, challenging certain aspects of EPA's revisions of the PM NAAQS as promulgated December 2006. A February 24, 2009, decision by the D.C. Circuit granted the petitions in part, denying other challenges, and remanded the standards to EPA for further consideration. The court did not specifically vacate the 2006 PM NAAQS and implementation is currently underway.

EPA received considerable (more than 230,000 written) comments in response to the June 2012 proposal. Concerned stakeholders may return to the courts or initiate challenges in response to the final standards published on January 15, 2013, thus potentially furthering delays in designating nonattainment areas, and states' development and implementation of SIPs.

---

[104] *Whitman v. American Trucking Associations*, 531 U.S. 457 (2001). Along with deciding issues specific to PM and ozone, the Court ruled unanimously that costs could not be considered in setting primary (health based) NAAQS.

Appendix A. Chronological Summary of Key Milestones Subsequent to the January 2013 PM NAAQS Final Rule

As part of the D.C. Circuit's decision and a related Consent Agreement, EPA agreed to issue final revised PM NAAQS by December 14, 2012. The timeline presented in **Table A-1** below reflects the most recent projected milestone dates subsequent to the January 15, 2013, publication of the final rule revising the PM NAAQS. These milestones are driven primarily by statutory requirements under the CAA, and are based on milestones identified in the June 29, 2012, *Federal Register* and EPA fact sheets accompanying the agency's proposed and final regulatory actions. The CAA does not specify a timeframe with regard to when states must meet secondary PM standards; relevant milestones are determined by EPA and states through the implementation planning process.

Table A-1. Milestone Chronology for Actions Subsequent to the January 2013 Final Revisions to the PM NAAQS

Actual and Projected Date	January 2013 Revised PM NAAQS Milestones
December 14, 2012, Final Rule Released (F.R. published on January 15, 2013)	The EPA Administrator signed the final rule on December 14, 2012, as per the D.C. Circuit June 2012 and as agreed to under a Consent Decree. The final rule was published in the F.R. on January 15, 2013.
January 2014 Proposal of Area Designations (required by CAA within one year after publication of PM NAAQS final rule)	State-tribal area designation recommendations (based on 2010-2012 monitoring data).
August-September 2014 EPA Response	EPA notifies states and tribes regarding modifications to their recommendations.
January 2015 Final Area Designations (required one year after states and tribes make recommendations)	EPA promulgates final area designations; expected effective data early 2015.
No Date Available (pending)	EPA proposes $PM_{2.5}$ implementation rule.
Early 2016 (one year after the final designation effective date of early 2015)	States with new transportation projects submit conformity determination within one year of the effective date of nonattainment designation.
Not Available	EPA promulgates final $PM_{2.5}$ implementation rule.
Early 2018 (3 years after final area designations effective date of January 15, 2013)	States and tribes are to submit revised implementation plans (SIPs) to achieve $PM_{2.5}$ compliance in nonattainment areas required three years after final designations.
Early 2020-2025 (5-10 years after final area designations effective date of January 15, 2013)	CAA NAAQS statutory compliance deadline that States must meet the health standards "as expeditiously as practicable" but not later than five years after designations. A state may request a possible extension to 2025, depending on the severity of an area's fine particle pollution problems and the availability of pollution controls.

Source: Prepared by CRS based on U.S. Environmental Protection Agency fact sheets, technical documents, guidance accompanying the EPA PM NAAQS final rule published on January 15, 2013, 77 *Federal Register* 38889-39055 , and the proposed rule, 77 *Federal Register* 38889-39055, June 29, 2012. See http://www.epa.gov/pm/actions.html.

Appendix B. Supporting EPA Scientific and Policy Documents, and CASAC Review

Table B-1. Chronological Listing of EPA Workshops, and Technical and Policy Documents in Support of the 2013 Revised PM NAAQS

Workshop/Draft or Final Document	Date
Integrated Science Assessment for Particulate Matter: Call for Information	June 2007
Workshop to Discuss Policy-Relevant Science to Inform EPA's Integrated Plan for the Review of the Primary PM NAAQS - Final Agenda	July 2007
Workshop to Discuss Policy-Relevant Science to Inform EPA's Integrated Plan for the Review of the Secondary PM NAAQS - Final Agenda	July 2007
PM NAAQS Integrated Review Plan - Draft	October 2007
PM NAAQS Integrated Review Plan - Final	March 2008
Notice of Workshop to Review Initial Draft Materials for the PM Integrated Science Assessment	May 2008
Integrated Science Assessment for Particulate Matter - First External Review Draft	December 2008
PM NAAQS: Scope and Methods Plan for Urban Visibility Impact Assessment	February 2009
PM NAAQS: Scope and Methods Plan for Health Risk and Exposure Assessment	February 2009
Integrated Science Assessment for Particulate Matter - Second External Review Draft	July 2009
Particulate Matter Urban-Focused Visibility Assessment—External Review Draft	September 2009
Risk Assessment to Support the Review of the PM Primary National Ambient Air Quality Standards - External Review Draft	September 2009
Review of Urban Visibility Public Preference Studies (Final Report)	September 2009
Urban-Focused Visibility Assessment Data File	November 2009
Corrections to Relative Humidity Values Used in the Draft UFVA, Corrected Graphics, Tables, and Availability of Detailed Data File for Current Conditions	November 2009
Integrated Science Assessment for PM (Final Report)	December 2009
Particulate Matter Urban-Focused Visibility Assessment - Second External Review Draft	January 2010
Statistical Analysis of Existing Urban Visibility Preference Studies	February 2010
Corrections to Relative Humidity Values Used in the Draft Urban-Focused Visibility Assessment, Availability of Data File Comparing Incorrect RH Data to Corrected RH Data for Atlanta and Birmingham	February 2010
Quantitative Health Risk Assessment for Particulate Matter—Second External Review Draft	February 2010
Revision to Section 3.3.5 of the Second External Review Draft of the PM Urban Visibility Assessment	March 2010
Analyses of PM2.5 Data for the PM NAAQS Review, Hassett-Sipple	March 2010
Quantitative Health Risk Assessment for Particulate Matter - Final Report	June 2010
Quantitative Health Risk Assessment for Particular Matter - Air Quality Data Files (for hybrid rollback-based analyses)	June 2010
Quantitative Health Risk Assessment for Particular Matter - Air Quality Data Files (for proportional and locally focused rollback-based analyses)	June 2010
Corrected Urban-Focused Visibility Assessment Data File	July 2010

Workshop/Draft or Final Document	Date
Particulate Matter Urban-Focused Visibility Assessment - Final Document	July 2010
PM10 and PM10-2.5 Air Quality Analyses, Schmidt and Jenkins	July 2010
Particulate Matter Air Quality Data Requested from Epidemiologic Study Authors	July 2010
SANDWICH-Related Correction to the UFVA Data File, as Used for the Final Document	July 2010
Explanation of Error in Table 4-3 of the Final UFVA	July 2010
PM2.5 Air Quality Analyses	July 2010
Assessment of the Use of Speciated PM2.5 Mass-Calculated Light Extinction as a Secondary PM NAAQS Indicator of Visibility	November 2010
Simplified Approaches for Calculation of Hourly PM2.5 Light Extinction Values From Hourly PM2.5 Mass and Relative Humidity Data and 24-hour PM2.5 Composition Data	November 2010
Supplemental analysis of PM10 Air Quality from Locations Evaluated by Zanobetti and Schwartz (2009)	February 2011
PM2.5 Air Quality Analyses - Update	April 2011
PM10 and PM10-2.5 Air Quality Analyses	April 2011
PM2.5 Distributional Statistical Analyses	April 2011
Assessment of PM2.5 FEMs Compared to Collocated FRMs	April 2011
Investigation of 1-hour PM2.5 Mass Concentration Data from EPA-Approved Continuous Federal Equivalent Method Analyzers	April 2011
Documentation of Measurement Uncertainty Estimates of Collocated Chemical Speciation Network and IMPROVE Data for Use in the Secondary PM2.5 Standard for Visibility	June 2012
Recommendations for Sampling Artifact Correction for PM2.5 Organic Carbon	June 2012
Technical Analyses to Support Surrogacy Policy for Proposed Secondary PM2.5 NAAQS under NSR/PSD Programs	June 2012

Source: Prepared by CRS based on U.S. Environmental Protection Agency fact sheets, list of technical documents available on its website Technology Transfer Network (TNN) National Ambient Air Quality Standards (NAAQS): Particulate Matter (PM) Standards—Documents from Current Review at http://www.epa.gov/ttn/naaqs/standards/pm/s_pm_index.html, and 77 *Federal Register* 38889-39055, June 29, 2012.

Table B-2. Chronological Listing of CASAC Reviews and Consultations

Review/Consultation	Date
CASAC Particulate Matter Review Panel's Consultation on EPA's Draft Integrated Review Plan for the National Ambient Air Quality Standards for Particulate Matter - Teleconference	November 2007
CASAC Particulate Matter Review Panel's Consultation on EPA's Draft Integrated Review Plan for the National Ambient Air Quality Standards for Particulate Matter - Report	January 2008
Consultation on Ambient Air Monitoring Issues Related to the Coarse Particle Speciation by the Clean Air Scientific Advisory Committee (CASAC) Ambient Air Monitoring & Methods Subcommittee (AAMMS)	March 2009
Review of EPA's Integrated Science Assessment for Particulate Matter (First External Review Draft December 2008)	May 2009
Consultation on EPA's Particulate Matter National Ambient Air Quality Standards: Scope and Methods Plan for Health Risk and Exposure Assessment	May 2009
Consultation on EPA's Particulate Matter National Ambient Air Quality Standards: Scope and Methods Plan for Urban Visibility Impact Assessment	May 2009
Review of Integrated Science Assessment for Particulate Matter (Second External Review Draft, July 2009)	November 2009
Review of Particulate Matter Urban-Focused Visibility Assessment (External Review Draft, September 2009)	November 2009
Review of Risk Assessment to Support the Review of the Particulate Matter (PM) Primary National Ambient Air Quality Standards—External Review Draft (September 2009)	November 2009
CASAC Review of Particulate Matter Urban-Focused Visibility Assessment—Second External Review Draft (January 2010)	April 2010
CASAC Review of Quantitative Health Risk Assessment for Particulate Matter—Second External Review Draft (February 2010)	April 2010
Review of the White Paper on Particulate Matter (PM) Light Extinction Measurements	April 2010
CASAC Review of Policy Assessment for the Review of the PM NAAQS—First External Review Draft (March 2010)	May 2010
CASAC Review of Policy Assessment for the Review of the PM NAAQS—Second External Review Draft (June 2010)	September 2010

Source: Prepared by CRS based on U.S. Environmental Protection Agency fact sheets, list of CASAC documents available on EPA's websites "EPA Clean Air Scientific Advisory Committee (CASAC) Final Reports by Topic" at http://yosemite.epa.gov/sab/sabproduct.nsf/WebReportsbyTopicCASAC!OpenView, and 77 *Federal Register* 38889-39055, June 29, 2012.

Appendix C. Comparison of Potential Nonattainment Areas for the January 2013 Final Revised PM₂.₅ Annual Standard with the Final Designations for the 2006 and 1997 PM₂.₅ NAAQS

Table C-1. Nonattainment Areas for the January 2013 24-Hour PM₂.₅ NAAQS as Estimated Using 2009-2011 Data, Final Designations 2006 24-Hour PM₂.₅ NAAQS October 8, 2009, and Final Designations for the 1997 PM₂.₅ NAAQS Annual

	1997 PM₂.₅ NAAQS	2006 PM₂.₅ NAAQS	2013 PM₂.₅ NAAQS
	EPA Final Designations **Annual Standard (15 µg/m³)**	**EPA Final Designations** **24-Hour Standard (35 µg/m³ 98ᵗʰ)**	**Proxy Designations (based on 2009-2011 Data)** **Annual Standard (12 µg/m³)**
Designation Areas		**Counties and Partial Counties (p)**	
ALABAMA			
Birmingham, AL[a]	Jefferson	Jefferson	Jefferson
	Shelby	Shelby	
	Walker (p)	Walker (p)	
Chattanooga, AL-TN-GA	Jackson (p)		
UNDEFINED[b]			Russell
ALASKA			
Fairbanks, AK		Fairbanks N. Star (p)	Fairbanks N. Star
ARIZONA			
Nogales, AZ			
Pinal, CA		Pinal (p) (designated February 3, 2011)[c]	
ARKANSAS			
UNDEFINED[b]			Pulaski
CALIFORNIA			
Chico, CA		Butte (p)	
Imperial County, CA		Imperial (p)	Imperial
Los Angeles, CA	Los Angeles (p)	Los Angeles (p)	Los Angeles
	Orange	Orange	
	Riverside (p)	Riverside (p)	Riverside
	San Bernardino (p)	San Bernardino (p)	San Bernardino

	1997 PM2.5 NAAQS	2006 PM2.5 NAAQS	2013 PM2.5 NAAQS
			Proxy Designations (based on 2009-2011 Data)
	EPA Final Designations	**EPA Final Designations**	
	Annual Standard (15 µg/m³)	**24-Hour Standard (35 µg/m³ 98th)**	**Annual Standard (12 µg/m³)**
Designation Areas		**Counties and Partial Counties (p)**	
Sacramento, CA		El Dorado (p)	
		Placer (p)	
		Sacramento	
		Solano (p)	
		Yolo (p)	
San Francisco Bay Area, CA		Alameda	
		Contra Costa	
		Marin	
		Napa	
		San Francisco	
		San Mateo	
		Santa Clara	
		Solano (p)	
		Sonoma (p)	
San Joaquin Valley, CA	Fresno	Fresno	Fresno
	Kern (p)	Kern (p)	Kern
	Kings	Kings	Kings
	Madera	Madera	
	Merced	Merced	Merced
	San Joaquin	San Joaquin	
	Stanislaus	Stanislaus	Stanislaus
	Tulare	Tulare	Tulare
Yuba City-Marysville, CA		Sutter	
		Yuba (p)	
CONNECTICUT			
New York, NY-NJ-CT	Fairfield	Fairfield	
	New Haven	New Haven	

	1997 PM₂.₅ NAAQS	2006 PM₂.₅ NAAQS	2013 PM₂.₅ NAAQS
	EPA Final Designations	**EPA Final Designations**	**Proxy Designations (based on 2009-2011 Data)**
	Annual Standard (15 µg/m³)	**24-Hour Standard (35 µg/m³ 98th)**	**Annual Standard (12 µg/m³)**
Designation Areas	**Counties and Partial Counties (p)**		
DELAWARE			
Philadelphia- Wilmington, PA-NJ-DE	New Castle	New Castle	
DISTRICT OF COLUMBIA			
Washington, DC-MD-VA	Entire District		
GEORGIA			
Atlanta, GA	Barrow		
	Bartow		
	Carroll		
	Cherokee		
	Clayton		Clayton
	Cobb		
	Coweta		
	De Kalb		
	Douglas		
	Fayette		
	Forsyth		
	Fulton		Fulton
	Gwinnett		
	Hall		
	Heard (p)		
	Henry		
	Newton		
	Paulding		
	Putnam (p)		
	Rockdale		
	Spalding		
	Walton		

	1997 PM₂.₅ NAAQS	2006 PM₂.₅ NAAQS	2013 PM₂.₅ NAAQS
	EPA Final Designations	**EPA Final Designations**	**Proxy Designations (based on 2009-2011 Data)**
	Annual Standard (15 μg/m³)	**24-Hour Standard (35 μg/m³ 98th)**	**Annual Standard (12 μg/m³)**
Designation Areas	Counties and Partial Counties (p)		
Chattanooga, AL-TN-GA	Catoosa		
	Walker		
Macon, GA	Bibb		Bibb
	Monroe (p)		
Rome, GA	Floyd		Floyd
UNDEFINED[b]			Dougherty
			Muscogee
			Richmond
			Wikinson
HAWAII			
UNDEFINED[b]			Hawaii
IDAHO			
Logan, UT-ID		Franklin (p)	
Pinehurst, ID			
ILLINOIS			
Chicago-Gary-Lake County, IL-IN	Cook		Cook
	DuPage		
	Grundy (p)		
	Kane		
	Kendall (p)		
	Lake		
	McHenry		
	Will		
St. Louis, MO-IL	Madison		Madison
	Monroe		
	Randolph (p)		
	St. Clair		St. Clair

	1997 PM₂.₅ NAAQS	2006 PM₂.₅ NAAQS	2013 PM₂.₅ NAAQS
	EPA Final Designations	**EPA Final Designations**	**Proxy Designations (based on 2009-2011 Data)**
	Annual Standard (15 μg/m³)	24-Hour Standard (35 μg/m³ 98th)	Annual Standard (12 μg/m³)
Designation Areas	**Counties and Partial Counties (p)**		
INDIANA			
Chicago-Gary-Lake County, IL-IN	Lake		
	Porter		
Cincinnati-Hamilton, OH-KY-IN	Dearborn (p)		
Evansville, IN	Dubois		Dubois
	Gibson (p)		
	Pike (p)		
	Spencer (p)		
	Vanderburgh		
	Warrick		
Indianapolis, IN	Hamilton		
	Hendricks		
	Johnson		
	Marion		Marion
	Morgan		
Lafayette-Frankfort, IN			
Louisville, KY-IN	Clark		Clark
	Floyd		Floyd
	Jefferson (p)		
Vincennes, IN			
UNDEFINED[b]			Lake
			Spencer
			Vanderbugh
			Vigo
IOWA			
Davenport-Moline-Rock Island, IA-IL			Scott
Muscatine, IA			Muscatine

	1997 PM$_{2.5}$ NAAQS	2006 PM$_{2.5}$ NAAQS	2013 PM$_{2.5}$ NAAQS
	EPA Final Designations	EPA Final Designations	Proxy Designations (based on 2009-2011 Data)
	Annual Standard (15 µg/m³)	24-Hour Standard (35 µg/m³ 98th)	Annual Standard (12 µg/m³)
Designation Areas	**Counties and Partial Counties (p)**		
KENTUCKY			
Cincinnati-Hamilton, OH-KY-IN	Boone		
	Campbell		
	Kenton		
Huntington-Ashland, WV-KY-OH	Boyd		
	Lawrence (p)		
Louisville, KY-IN	Bullitt		Bullitt
	Jefferson		Jefferson
Paducah-Mayfield, KY-IL			
UNDEFINED[b]			Daviess
MARYLAND			
Baltimore, MD	Anne Arundel		
	Baltimore City		
	Baltimore		
	Carroll		
	Harford		
	Howard		
Washington, DC-MD-VA	Charles		
	Frederick		
	Montgomery		
	Prince George's		
Martinsburg, WV- Hagerstown, MD	Washington		

	1997 PM$_{2.5}$ NAAQS	2006 PM$_{2.5}$ NAAQS	2013 PM$_{2.5}$ NAAQS
	EPA Final Designations	EPA Final Designations	Proxy Designations (based on 2009-2011 Data)
	Annual Standard (15 µg/m³)	24-Hour Standard (35 µg/m³ 98th)	Annual Standard (12 µg/m³)
Designation Areas	**Counties and Partial Counties (p)**		
MICHIGAN			
Detroit-Ann Arbor, MI	Livingston	Livingston	
	Macomb	Macomb	
	Monroe	Monroe	
	Oakland	Oakland	
	St. Clair	St. Clair	
	Washtenaw	Washtenaw	
	Wayne	Wayne	
Grand Rapids, MI			
MISSISSIPPI			
MISSOURI			
St. Louis, MO-IL	Franklin		
	Jefferson		
	St. Charles		
	St. Louis		
	St. Louis City		St. Louis City
MONTANA			
Libby, MT	Lincoln (p)		
NEW JERSEY			
New York, NY-NJ-CT	Bergen		
	Essex		
	Hudson		
	Mercer		
	Middlesex		
	Monmouth		
	Morris		
	Passaic	Passaic	
	Somerset	Somerset	
	Union	Union	

	1997 PM₂.₅ NAAQS	2006 PM₂.₅ NAAQS	2013 PM₂.₅ NAAQS
	EPA Final Designations	**EPA Final Designations**	**Proxy Designations (based on 2009-2011 Data)**
	Annual Standard (15 µg/m³)	**24-Hour Standard (35 µg/m³ 98ᵗʰ)**	**Annual Standard (12 µg/m³)**
Designation Areas	**Counties and Partial Counties (p)**		
Philadelphia- Wilmington, PA-NJ-DE	Burlington	Burlington	
	Camden	Camden	
	Gloucester	Gloucester	
NEW YORK			
New York, NY-NJ-CT	Bronx	Bronx	
	Kings	Kings	
	Nassau	Nassau	
	New York	New York	
	Orange	Orange	
	Queens	Queens	
	Richmond	Richmond	
	Rockland	Rockland	
	Suffolk	Suffolk	
	Westchester	Westchester	
NORTH CAROLINA			
Hickory, NC	Catawba		
Greensboro-Winston Salem-High Point, NC	Davidson		
	Guilford		
UNDEFINED			
OHIO			
Canton-Massillon, OH	Stark	Stark	
Cincinnati-Hamilton, OH-KY-IN	Butler		Butler
	Clermont		
	Hamilton		Hamilton
	Warren		

	1997 PM$_{2.5}$ NAAQS	2006 PM$_{2.5}$ NAAQS	2013 PM$_{2.5}$ NAAQS
	EPA Final Designations	EPA Final Designations	Proxy Designations (based on 2009-2011 Data)
	Annual Standard (15 µg/m³)	24-Hour Standard (35 µg/m³ 98th)	Annual Standard (12 µg/m³)
Designation Areas	**Counties and Partial Counties (p)**		
Cleveland-Akron- Lorain, OH	Ashtabula (p)		
	Cuyahoga	Cuyahoga	Cuyahoga
	Lake	Lake	
	Lorain	Lorain	
	Medina	Medina	
	Portage	Portage	
	Summit	Summit	Summit
Columbus, OH	Coshocton (p)		
	Delaware		
	Fairfield		
	Franklin		Franklin
	Licking		
Dayton-Springfield, OH	Clark		Clark
	Greene		
	Montgomery		Montgomery
Huntington-Ashland, WV-KY-OH	Adams (p)		
	Gallia (p)		
	Lawrence		
	Scioto		
Parkersburg- Marietta, WV-OH	Washington		
Steubenville- Weirton, OH-WV	Jefferson	Jefferson	Jefferson
Wheeling, WV-OH	Belmont		
Youngstown, OH			

	1997 PM₂.₅ NAAQS	2006 PM₂.₅ NAAQS	2013 PM₂.₅ NAAQS
	EPA Final Designations	**EPA Final Designations**	**Proxy Designations (based on 2009-2011 Data)**
	Annual Standard (15 μg/m³)	**24-Hour Standard (35 μg/m³ 98th)**	**Annual Standard (12 μg/m³)**
Designation Areas		**Counties and Partial Counties (p)**	
OREGON			
Klamath Falls, OR		Klamath (p)	
Oakridge, OR		Lane (p)	
PENNSYLVANIA			
Allentown, PA		Lehigh	
		Northampton	Northampton
Harrisburg-Lebanon-Carlisle, PA		Cumberland	
		Dauphin	
		Lebanon	Dauphin
		York	
Johnstown, PA	Cambria	Cambria	Cambria
	Indiana (p)	Indiana (p)	
Lancaster, PA	Lancaster	Lancaster	
Liberty-Clairton, PA	Allegheny (p)	Allegheny (p)	Allegheny
Philadelphia-Wilmington, PA-NJ-DE	Bucks	Bucks	
	Chester	Chester	Chester
	Delaware	Delaware	Delaware
	Montgomery	Montgomery	
	Philadelphia	Philadelphia	
Pittsburgh-Beaver Valley, PA	Allegheny (p)	Allegheny (p)	Allegheny
	Armstrong (p)	Armstrong (p)	
	Beaver	Beaver	Beaver
	Butler	Butler	
	Greene (p)	Greene (p)	
	Lawrence (p)	Lawrence (p)	
	Washington	Washington	Washington
	Westmoreland	Westmoreland	Westmoreland
Reading, PA	Berks		
York, PA	York		

	1997 PM$_{2.5}$ NAAQS	2006 PM$_{2.5}$ NAAQS		2013 PM$_{2.5}$ NAAQS
	EPA Final Designations	**EPA Final Designations**		**Proxy Designations (based on 2009-2011 Data)**
	Annual Standard (15 µg/m³)	**24-Hour Standard (35 µg/m³ 98th)**		**Annual Standard (12 µg/m³)**
Designation Areas		**Counties and Partial Counties (p)**		
TENNESSEE				
Chattanooga, AL-TN-GA	Hamilton			
Clarksville, TN-KY				
Knoxville-Sevierville- La Follette, TN	Anderson	Anderson		
	Blount	Blount		
	Knox	Knox		Knox
	Loudon	Loudon		
	Roane (p)	Roane (p)		
TEXAS				
UNDEFINED[b]				Harris
UTAH				
Logan, UT-ID		Cache (p)		
Provo, UT		Utah (p)		
Salt Lake City, UT		Box Elder (p)		
		Davis		
		Salt Lake		
		Tooele (p)		
		Weber (p)		
VIRGINIA				
Washington, DC-MD-VA	Alexandria City			
	Arlington			
	Fairfax City			
	Fairfax Co			
	Falls Church City			
	Loudoun			

	1997 PM$_{2.5}$ NAAQS	2006 PM$_{2.5}$ NAAQS	2013 PM$_{2.5}$ NAAQS
	EPA Final Designations	EPA Final Designations	Proxy Designations (based on 2009-2011 Data)
	Annual Standard (15 µg/m³)	24-Hour Standard (35 µg/m³ 98th)	Annual Standard (12 µg/m³)
Designation Areas	Counties and Partial Counties (p)		
	Manassas City		
	Manassas Park City		
	Prince William		
WASHINGTON			
Seattle-Tacoma, WA		Pierce (p)	
WEST VIRGINIA			
Charleston, WV	Kanawha	Kanawha	Kanawha
	Putnam	Putnam	
Huntington-Ashland, WV-KY-OH	Cabell		Cabell
	Mason (p)		
	Wayne		
Martinsburg, WV-Hagerstown, MD	Berkeley		
Morgantown, WV			
Parkersburg- Marietta, WV-OH	Pleasants (p)		
	Wood		Wood
Steubenville- Weirton, OH-WV	Brooke	Brooke	Brooke
	Hancock	Hancock	Hancock
Wheeling, WV-OH	Marshall		Marshall
	Ohio		Ohio
UNDEFINED[b]			Marion
WISCONSIN			
Green Bay, WI			
Madison-Baraboo, WI			
Milwaukee-Racine, WI		Milwaukee	
		Racine	
		Waukesha	

	1997 PM$_{2.5}$ NAAQS	2006 PM$_{2.5}$ NAAQS	2013 PM$_{2.5}$ NAAQS
	EPA Final Designations	EPA Final Designations	Proxy Designations (based on 2009-2011 Data)
	Annual Standard (15 µg/m³)	24-Hour Standard (35 µg/m³ 98th)	Annual Standard (12 µg/m³)
Designation Areas		**Counties and Partial Counties (p)**	
		TOTALS	
	20 states and DC	18 states	16 states
	38 areas	31 areas	NA
	204 counties	120 counties	66 counties
	173 whole counties	90 whole counties	NA
	31 partial counties	30 partial counties	NA

Source: Compiled by CRS using data from EPA Fact Sheets accompanying the January 15, 2013, final PM NAAQS rule, and EPA PM Designation's websites. In some designated areas, EPA included cities in the total count of whole and partial counties, with the exception of the District of Columbia.

a. In the September 20, 2010, *Federal Register*, EPA announced its determination that a three-county (Jefferson, Shelby, and portion of Walker) Alabama nonattainment area (Birmingham) has attaining data for the 2006 24-hour PM$_{2.5}$ NAAQS (75 *Federal Register* 57186, September 20, 2010). The clean air data determination was based on certified ambient air monitoring data showing the area monitored as in attainment for the 2006 24-hour PM$_{2.5}$ NAAQS based on 2007-2009 data.

b. The "designated areas" including one or more counties (or portions of counties) are as defined in the final designations for the 2006 PM$_{2.5}$. Those counties identified as potential nonattainment areas for the January 2013 revised standards that were not part of previously defined PM$_{2.5}$ NAAQS designated areas are characterized as "UNDEFINED" designation areas.

c. In a February 3, 2011 final notice, EPA published designations of three areas as "nonattainment" or "unclassifiable/attainment" for the 2006 24-PM$_{2.5}$ NAAQS that were deferred in the November 13, 2009, promulgated designations, 76 *Federal Register* 6056-6066, http://www.epa.gov/pmdesignations/2006standards/documents/2011-01/FR-2011-01.pdf.

d. In the August 25, 2008, *Federal Register*, EPA announced its determination that a three-county (Harrisburg, Lebanon, Carlisle) Pennsylvania nonattainment area for the 1997 PM$_{2.5}$ NAAQS was in attainment (73 *Federal Register* 49949, August 25, 2008). The determination was based on certified ambient air monitoring data showing the area monitored as in attainment for the 1997 PM$_{2.5}$ NAAQS since the 2004-2006 monitoring period.

Author Contact Information

Robert Esworthy
Specialist in Environmental Policy
resworthy@crs.loc.gov, 7-7236

www.ingramcontent.com/pod-product-compliance
Lightning Source LLC
Chambersburg PA
CBHW080616290526
45790CB00007B/2807